DRAGON'S PLAY

DRAGON'S PLAY

A New Taoist Transmission of the Complete Experience of Human Life

Charles Belyea *and* **Steven Tainer**

Illustrations by Xiao-Lun Lin

Great Circle Lifeworks
Berkeley

DRAGON'S PLAY

For information address
Great Circle Lifeworks, 1419 Walnut St., Berkeley, CA 94709.

9 8 7 6 5 4 3 2 1
First Edition

Library of Congress Catalog Card Number 91-72597

ISBN 0-9629308-1-4

Cover / Xiao-Lun Lin
Typesetting / Byron Brown

To
the Living Universe

Acknowledgments

Linda Ankenny, Monisha Alleck, Diane Byrd,
Ron Zaidman, Joanna Zhao, Rob and Cathy Calef,
Joui Corradini, Sally Lewis, Neil Shaffron, Paul and
Nancy Clemens, Ralph Moon, Richard Stodart,
Ken Pearlman, Glen Farell, and Alicia Sarzoza-Tainer

CONTENTS

PREFACE

[ST] When I first met Charles, he had just emerged from a one-year solitary retreat. I immediately saw that he embodied the lightness and relaxed accommodation of humanness that are so vital to effective cultivation and communication of life's 'spiritual' dimensions. So I urged him to teach this Way he'd brought back from China in the 1970's.

[CB] It had always been kept 'secret' in the past ... or perhaps 'discrete' is a better word ... so I was a bit hesitant at first. But my own masters in Taiwan had encouraged me to make it available, not as a sect but as a resource for anyone willing to practice self respect and to enjoy life directly. So in this book, we lay the groundwork for a full transmission of this teaching.

[ST] Initially—in the early Eighty's—we were concentrating on writing about the rather advanced yogic methods of this lineage.

[CB] We eventually realized that the teachings require a nontechnical style of presentation, and that a complete picture of the human situation was needed as a foundation. This lightness and View is quite traditional for my lineage.

[ST] So we agreed to set our first writings on Taoist yogic methods aside until we could offer a framework for putting them and ordinary human life in perspective. As it happened, no sooner did we decide that than Charles drew this twelve-stage story from his own experience.

[CB] The book's story has its roots in some very incisive points made by one of my teachers. He stressed in various ways that the essence of Taoism was what works for people, what is natural and humane ... "no fighting or narrowness." In 1983, I looked into the implications of his vision, and discovered a truly modern teaching that encompassed the old tradition. And by then, it was definitely 'eager' to come out. I tested it in public presentations, and later wrote it in summary form while resting one afternoon during a retreat with Steven in the Sierras.

[ST] I had the impression that he was simply writing what he saw, so there wasn't any thought or effort required, nothing to 'develop.' In the years that followed, we explored this teaching together in great depth and then wrote the full text in 1989 (the Year of the Dragon).

[CB] Our situation was an ironic reminder of my experience in Taiwan—my teachers had joked that instead of adding a 'last' chapter to their technical meditation manuals, as is traditional for a new lineage holder, I would end up producing the hitherto 'unwritten' first book of the set.

[ST] This is both the first text of the old lineage and also a new teaching for a new time. And in order to offer a new teaching, Charles had to go back to the Source of the old one, to the "origin of the original" teaching. He has also emphasized that each of us must do that in order to make these teachings come to life. The point was not to invent something new or popularize something ancient, but to return to the plain root.

[CB] Right, because only then can you see what is essential and bring that, without extra or outdated trappings, directly into the experience of the modern world. Even before I first went to China, I was musing over this issue, never imagining how importantly it would figure in my life. By luck or fate, in Taiwan I was able to study with a particular family lineage, connected with the original sect of Taoist yoga.

[ST] We'll present the full story of this training in other books.

[CB] Later I also was able to return to and be deeply 'moved' by the original place of that lineage (on Mount Ching Cheng in Sichuan). And the most important point is indeed to return to the "original experience" that motivated all the later historical developments, to teach from that. Finally, I worked with Steven in a traditionally Taoist, personal way to retrace these steps for him, to find the origin that spoke to both of us.

[ST] That personal interaction was also part of the lineage's original emphasis—going out to where the original experience is most founded and relevant in the lives of other people ... people such as myself and Charles's students, but also those of you reading Dragon's Play. Both learning and offering the teaching should be based on the "making friends" image which is at the very heart of this book.

[CB] It's so important to make friends with ourselves, and with the situations and people figuring in our lives. The vision presented here may both assist that and in turn be further clarified by it. The inherent 'Dragon' energies of life will then be harmonized and released to their full, playful and creative scope.

INTRODUCTION

This book summarizes and comments extensively on some ancient Taoist teaching stories—actually the precursors to the well-known Zen Oxherding pictures. It is also related in spirit to Chinese folk novels like the popular *Monkey*, from the *Journey to the West (Hsi Yu Ki)*. Inspired by our own Taoist teachers and the rich ground of Chinese literature, our story looks out over human nature and human life, celebrating their place in Nature.

We refer here to a living Nature, which nurtures human engagements but resists being reduced to human assessments. Such an appreciation of Nature is very ancient, virtually 'primordial.' We hope to make the full import of this view accessible again in a time preoccupied with other issues.

Considered in much more specific terms, *Dragon's Play* presents a direct and natural view of meditation, yoga, and what Taoists call "cultivating the Way." It's not about Taoism specifically, although it is founded on study with Taoist masters in China and extensive practice of Taoist methods. It does offer a view which is consistent with some central ideas of Taoism, and refers at times to Taoist insights and terms to illustrate certain points.

Rather than concentrating on explaining any particular sect or tradition, our purpose is to describe "cultivating the Way" as a central agenda of human life. Instead of emphasizing achievements and special experiences, we stress the importance of determining where we are, where life is going, and how it may unfold to its fullest extent.

The most sane and potent answers to these questions come from connecting to our basic living nature and acknowledging our place in Nature. It's more important for people to find and appreciate themselves than it is to undergo change or focus on exotic experiences.

OUR RELATIONSHIP TO NATURE

The human relationship to Nature is necessarily the central theme, and it is because this point was understood and explored in a wide variety of ways by Taoists, without being reduced to dogma, that we draw on Taoism in our presentation. The Taoist exploration of this issue is particularly rich, since it was conducted within the supporting environment of three thousand years of human culture in China.

During that enormous span of time, various insights came to the fore and the relevance of many different aspects of the human relationship to Nature became evident. Taoist investigators tested them all to see where they fit, and assimilated them if their connection to the central theme was significant.

This accommodating attitude laid Taoists open to criticism by scholars more concerned with pure philosophy and narrow or idealized standards of progress than with the complete picture of the real human situation. Nevertheless, it is precisely the emphasis on free experimentation and on the full story of humanness, as it actually is, that makes Taoism a resource for everyone. Thus, we too take up the task of sounding out the full human terrain and noting its place in the larger scheme of things.

As cultivators of the Way, we must all live through and accept the entire range of what is human, rather than trying to overcome it. We must also realize in the process that we are contextual creatures—our lives and aspirations are defined and supported by relationships, and specifically by relationships with Nature. Transcending humanness or Nature is impossible, even meaningless.

Once we appreciate our position, we can participate knowingly in the richness of the connection between human nature and Nature itself.

Escaping into "super-Natural" realms is just moving into fantasies or incomplete understandings of our experience and capabilities.

THE IMPORTANCE OF THE VIEW

Incomplete or biased views essentially send meditation off in a different direction from ordinary life, and hinder them both. A complete view enables them to converge, and makes them easy, joyous, free, and fiercely expressive activities—what we call "Dragon's Play." In this book, the image of the Dragon is used to represent the full functioning of basic human components, not something transcendent.

The fruit of meditation and life is to enjoy the human relationship to Nature, and we are already in that fruit. Moreover, the operation of this relationship provides the only motive power needed for all ordinary or extraordinary cultivations and demonstrations of the profundity of life.

Both ordinary and extraordinary demonstrations are entirely sufficient, so each person may choose them based on his or her individual interests. A good overview of our situation enables us to use various meditative technologies to travel far, if we wish. However, it also enables us to relax and appreciate remaining "at home."

"PATH LITERATURE"

Many books on meditative techniques are currently available, but few—if any—really explain what these techniques have to do with human nature and Nature. Because of that omission, they fail to provide an accurate map of where meditation can go and why, what happens along the way, what to emphasize and cultivate, who or what the cultivator really is, what to watch out for, and even what the real point of all this 'cultivation' might be.

Some traditional path literature has already been translated into Western languages, but we must question the aptness of much of it. For, it often itemizes and recommends exits from humanness, rather than providing maps into humanness. To take a common example, in perusing this literature one often reads about processes of "progressive refinement"—the practitioner wrestles with his or her thoughts or emotions or physical promptings, and eventually 'masters' them. The practitioner then learns to remain in states of absorption or composure undisturbed by normal thoughts or sensations of any sort, and extends the duration of these states to span hours, then days, etc.

At the end of such heroic courses in self-improvement, one supposedly transcends human limitations and mentation altogether, and enters new spheres of existence. Each such sphere, in turn, corresponds to a successively more extraordinary state of awareness, which has a technical name, etc.

One can become quite familiar with such literature and lists of states of attainment, without gaining any insight at all on the basic human situation—it's just something being left behind! Some people may indeed successfully cultivate the Way by traveling in the direction of such achievements and states, etc. But we intend to show that— far from being the central and generally recommended approach— it is rather tangential. It overlooks much that is really worth cultivating and understanding about humanness and the fruit of human life.

A different sort of view is needed, not just for specialists in meditation but for everyone. It's a matter of simple self respect.

TECHNICAL METHODS OF CULTIVATION

We will discuss six very potent yogic and contemplative methods in other books (and in the process we'll completely 'unpack' the Eight Heavenly Gates tradition of orthodox yogic Taoism). In those works we will show how seminal and profound methods can be linked to ordinary life and to what the Zen master Suzuki Roshi liked to call "beginner's mind" in his excellent book *Zen Mind, Beginner's Mind*. Such presentations of methods presuppose a balanced and complete view as the first priority, and we have attempted to provide that in the present book.

Methods should be understood as ways of demonstrating and living in the view, and become toxic when practiced out of context or as means to some fruit other than life itself. This book therefore provides a framework for grounding methods in general, not just those of our own lineage.

Beyond that, we hope to focus on the actual conduct of life, rather than encouraging a dependency on techniques. For as we move toward the Twenty-First century, it seems increasingly unlikely that circumstances will support the kind of concerted practice of highly specialized contemplative methods that characterized earlier times. If cultivating the Way truly involves celebrating and acting in accordance with the human relationship to Nature, it must realistically reflect the actual phases of both Nature and human nature that are now in ascendance.

NOTES ON STRUCTURE, CONTENT, AND USE

Dragon's Play is divided into two parts. Part I offers a basic outline of the twelve main facets of the human landscape. Each facet is introduced by a representative illustration, painted to our specifications by the Chinese calligrapher Xiao-Lun Lin. We refer to such illustrations as 'Images.' In Part I, each Image is accompanied on the facing page by an explanatory paragraph. Below that paragraph, another short discussion follows, summing up the 'lesson' learned at that particular juncture.

Part II presents an extended commentary of the same twelve facets, one per chapter. In each chapter, individual lines from the summary discussion in Part I are repeated (in italics) and then considered at some length. We recommend that you become familiar with the general scheme presented in Part I before moving on to Part II.

In both Parts, the twelve facets are arranged in the same sequence and are often referred to by their numbers (ONE, TWO, SEVEN, etc.). We might say that ONE represents a somewhat raw and small view of human existence, while TWELVE describes what Taoists call the Return to the Source, the fullest and deepest entry into the human

5

relationship to Nature. However, a few words about this notion of a definite sequence are in order.

Myths and ancient doctrines sometimes place the Source or Origin of the universe at the temporal beginning of things. And they go on to link the spiritual path with a return to that original Source, reversing the trend into manifestation and distinctions which bind the senses, create troubling dualisms, etc. This is a rather simple view, and does not *literally* describe the human situation and meditative agenda.

There really is no one Beginning, nor a cosmic or personal fall from grace. The path of Returning to the Source is not a matter of going back to the womb or transcending the diverse universe of manifestation. The Source is the context for everything. It's quite simply where we all are, and Returning to it means giving more attention to it as the basis for a full exploration of life.

Cultivating the Way of Returning to the Source doesn't mean escaping from ONE, journeying through intermediate stages, and finally taking refuge in TWELVE. It's a matter of seeing how many facets of life we—like the Source—can include and embrace.

The twelve facets are thoroughly discussed here because they're all 'true' and should all be appreciated. There is a natural movement running from ONE to TWELVE, and in one through six this movement does look like a trend toward advancement, a matter of scaling a mountain, so we call these facets Stages in our text. But as the second six Stages show, this is not simply the story of a journey or an account of personal improvement.

Each Stage is actually connected to every other, and these connections represent the Source's character of opening to the entire human landscape. So, our story is rather different from the usual, achievement-oriented path literature, which concludes with some sort of "peak experience" or transcendence of the world. TWELVE is not at the top of any mountain and is not a "peak experience"—that rather limited view exhausts itself long before TWELVE.

Since the Stages are really a continuous tapestry, connecting every which way, you may also read the chapters in Part II in various orders, as you please. We do, however, recommend at least a preliminary reading in the standard sequence, perhaps skipping those sections which go into more detail than you initially require.

The first six Stages will probably be familiar to you in many ways, so following Part II's treatment of them should seem simple and fun. But Stages Seven through Twelve are inherently more subtle. Reading the corresponding chapters may therefore require careful consideration at times.

Wherever possible, we have used simple language to discuss matters which traditionally have been kept secret, described only in very technical terms, or presented in veiled or metaphorical ways. Moreover, we have chosen our words to reflect direct, concrete experience. Nevertheless, the later chapters will probably be best understood after several readings and self-reflection and concentration on your own experience.

Please note that a full treatment of the 'later' Stages would require volumes of discussion, so we are necessarily skimming through the critical issues. Our other books will examine some of these points at greater length and show how they relate to specific systems of practice.

ON CULTIVATING THE WAY

Since this is not a book which emphasizes or teaches the use of meditative techniques, it might seem that the insights we discuss must remain elusive. But in fact, you don't need complex techniques to plunge into the heart of the Way. Also, if you understand and use the view we describe, you may utilize techniques from many different disciplines to cultivate the Way. On the other hand, without the view, the application of techniques becomes an endless and probably fruitless process, a preoccupation rather than true cultivation.

If, as you read Parts I and II, you find yourself thinking "Well this sounds fine, but how do I produce or achieve such an insight?," just focus on the basic point—nothing needs to be *produced* but only *found* where it's actually already happening!

Each of the characters described in ONE through TWELVE represents a facet of every human being and of the human relationship to Nature. These characters include a Monkey, Sage, various types of Immortals, and even a Dragon. All are aspects of you and your situation, and all are functioning now. They are in life, and are the real cultivators of the Way. Sometimes we also refer to a 'yogi,' which is just another way of talking about your real nature, entering into more and more central and unified experiences of itself.

Whether you use this view to facilitate daily life or to ground the practice of meditation, both clarity and confusion are accommodated within it. So even when you feel uncertain, it still places you in the fruit of cultivating the Way.

It is a privilege for us to make this gesture in defense of self respect and the appreciation of life, and we sincerely hope you find it useful.

PART 1

TWELVE FACETS OF
OUR RELATIONSHIP
TO NATURE

ONE ... DISCOVERING MONKEY

IMAGE: REFLECTION

At ONE Monkey is alone, perched on the branches of his small tree world, oblivious to the larger field of experience on which his very existence is grounded. His environment is a blur of the frantic activity created by unchecked desire. His erratic movements, full of uneasiness and paranoia, leave him breathless. In this limited fantasy world he is sometimes clever and amusing, but his overall experience of life is claustrophobic.

LESSON

"Discovering Monkey" must be the first experience in the self-reflection of a Cultivator of the Way. When—in the simple exercise of natural concentration—we find the repetitive cycle of self-deception and chaos, it is possible to honestly acknowledge the galling limitations of a life based on desire alone. In this moment of disenchantment, TWO appears.

TWO ... MONKEY MEETS SAGE

IMAGE: DUALITY

At TWO Monkey comes face to face with Sage. Sage is another vantage point within a new and enlarged environment. The two figures,
however, are 'frozen' in the duality of mutual self-discovery. They primarily dwell upon comparisons and labeling. Monkey views Sage as
idealistic and impractical. Sage views Monkey as selfish and unprin-
cipled. But all this judgment and labeling produce no real advantage.

LESSON

"Monkey meets Sage" is the discovery of the multi-faceted character of our nature. For the Cultivator of the Way this is no place to
stop—self-assessment for its own sake must be relinquished if the Way
is to open further. As we relax the paralytic pattern of judgment at
TWO, the journey of THREE is activated.

THREE ... JOURNEYING TOGETHER

IMAGE: TOLERANCE

At THREE Monkey leaves the confines of his tree world as he and Sage agree to begin a journey together. They turn their backs on the fruitless judgments of TWO, and venture forward in their new and expanding environment. Also at THREE, the ground becomes a more prominent aspect of the picture, representing the growing depth and solidity of Monkey and Sage's relationship. This emerging ground is the basis of their journey.

LESSON

"Journeying Together" involves natural concentration, based on simple self-acceptance and tolerance. This attitude creates a larger context in which apparently disparate aspects of ourselves may willingly join together on a mutual ground. Such tolerance may now also extend to others, further enhancing our cultivation. The Path awaits and we're able to embrace it as it is—no other inspiration is required for FOUR to become apparent.

FOUR ... EMBARKING ON THE WAY

IMAGE: KNOWLEDGE

At FOUR Monkey and Sage come upon a Path that cuts through a rich and varied new environment. They sense that their journey now contains elements of a destiny, and their confidence grows. They also feel what they must do. This new environment stimulates many insights that clarify their intentions. However, despite their continued cooperation, their apparent uniqueness and individuality are not yet diminished. Sage, still full of spiritual idealism, prepares himself for a noble commitment to a great Quest. Monkey, as hungry as ever, imagines great epicurean delights at the end of their journey.

LESSON

Knowledge and innocence characterize "Embarking on the Way." A Cultivator of the Way may, in innocence, consider the many insights available here as the fruit or goal of cultivation. For, no other goal has yet been identified. What is most important, however, is that we begin to grow up. Intoxication with the richness of knowledge at FOUR does not serve true cultivation. Our new intelligence and maturity must be applied to continue our journey, and vigorous action must be taken to find the maps and paths associated with the territory of FIVE.

FIVE ... REACHING THE MOUNTAIN

IMAGE: DISCRIMINATING ACTION

At FIVE Sage and Monkey find themselves on higher ground, with a broad view to the distant mountains. The central peak, promising a still larger vista, becomes their goal. Now that the goal seems clear, they feel greatly inspired and strengthened. However, the path at their feet splits into countless trails leading through vast expanses of uncharted territory. They may encounter 'tigers' here and, where possible, should avoid waking them. They must therefore choose carefully and intelligently from the many paths available, come to grips with unknown and powerful forces without entering into conflict, and continue their journey to the summit.

LESSON

"Reaching the Mountain" is a test of the Cultivator's maturity. The ground of our cultivation has risen to become a mountain, signifying both a greatly-enlarged experience of our basic nature and the corresponding need for increased vigor in encompassing it. This new panorama offers many options, so FIVE can be a place of overwhelming "spiritual consumerism." Some of the paths available are well-trodden and traditional, lined with helpful 'maps' or guides. Others are 'direct' in a person-specific sense, but unmarked and precipitous. Each Cultivator of the Way must understand his own unique nature enough to make appropriate choices. For, without the experience of ONE through FOUR, FIVE becomes a confusing tangle of possibilities, diverting us from proceeding to the summit at SIX.

19

SIX ... CLOUDLESS SUMMIT

IMAGE: END OF EFFORT

At SIX Monkey and Sage have reached their apparent goal. Now effort ends and all innocence about the real nature of cultivation is lost in the face of a truly panoramic vision. This environment contains no sustenance or support for them as 'Monkey' and 'Sage,' and they know they cannot stay long. To continue, they must transform themselves—that is, they must "let go" to something other than what they've always believed themselves to be. And indeed, the wind blows up from below and beckons them to 'fly' onward. Their insights are now all-encompassing and their compassion toward others is very great. However, the very intensity of their experience begins to burn them up, initiating the alchemical process that 'distills' or exposes their common, essential nature.

LESSON

When the "Cloudless Summit" is reached, efforts cease and we are confronted with the reality that cultivating the Way produces Nothing. The goal is not produced by the method, any more than the summit is produced by the journey. Once-treasured insights and inspiring vistas seem empty and flat in view of the panorama now before us. Only an effortless and absolute release satisfies us, opening to SEVEN.

SEVEN ... 'ATTAINING' THE WAY

IMAGE: SPACE

The empty frame at SEVEN shows a limitless Space, defying any definite depiction. Monkey, Sage, and the Mountain are now one with Space. This is the motionless open Space which includes all phenomena before, during, and after their myriad manifestations.

LESSON

"Attaining the Way" is the merger of our self-nature and Nature Itself, without death or transformation. Here the True Cultivator of the Way sees the basic functioning of life itself as cultivation, for we can no longer make a meaningful distinction between phenomena and this open Space. We now embark on a vast new journey, in which we must swim among the currents of Nature to fulfill our birth and completely demonstrate our true nature. We thus effortlessly approach EIGHT.

EIGHT ... THE LAWS OF NATURE

IMAGE: NATURAL ORDER

The Image of EIGHT is a symbolic depiction of the true and fundamental patterns of energy which constitute the Laws of Nature. They
are difficult to understand completely and yet operate freely within
us, ordering and reordering our relationship to Nature.

LESSON

Recognizing the "Laws of Nature" and all their operations allows the
True Cultivator of the Way to move among the currents of the Law
(Energy) without the inhibitions brought about by identification
with any particular entity, phenomenon, or event. This level of
experience is also associated with the natural emergence of yogic
meridians or channels through which the True Cultivator may proceed to 'generate' the energy characterizing NINE.

NINE ... ORIGINATING ENERGY

IMAGE: INFLUENCE

NINE is shown as a star-filled, luminous sky above mountains and cliffs overlooking the waves lapping on a seashore. The Image depicts the subtle movement and power of Nature, as well as the continuous transformations of its forms. Originating Energy is represented here as the influence of Heavenly Bodies on the phenomenal world.

LESSON:

The True Cultivator of the Way must master Nature's Originating Energy if he is to complete his full Return to the Source. At NINE, cultivation is characterized by the urge to demonstrate EIGHT through creative and playful experiments in the phenomenal world, consummating in Immortality at TEN.

TEN ... THE EARTHLY HSIEN

IMAGE: EMERGENCE

At TEN, the Earthly Immortal (Hsien) emerges fully mature, dancing in response to the currents of Earthly energy that surround him. The movements of his dance are spontaneous but highly instructive to all beings who encounter him. He simply eats when hungry, sleeps when tired, and plays when inspired, yet the profundity of such activity reverberates like thunder over the Earth.

LESSON

The Earthly Hsien is a man of action. The entire drama of ONE through NINE now emerges as an exercise of consummate ordinariness. It is essential that the True Cultivator of the Way avoid tying himself up in knots of cosmic seriousness. The Great Order of the universe was as apparent on Monkey's tree as it is now in the Immortal's dance, and a Return to ordinariness here exposes the freedom to enter a new, truly universal level of action at ELEVEN.

ELEVEN ... THE HEAVENLY HSIEN

IMAGE: MUTABILITY

At ELEVEN the Heavenly Hsien brings forth the infinite possibilities of Being in the form of an egg seated in the first Heavenly Chamber of his body. The seemingly ordinary activity of TEN has refined his Earthly form into the pure components of Nature, allowing him to manifest any or all things under Heaven.

LESSON

'Mutability' is the capacity of the True Cultivator of the Way to be at one with Nature in all of its manifest forms. All limits are gone and no vestige of gain, loss or a "spiritual agenda" can be found.

TWELVE ... RETURN TO THE SOURCE

IMAGE: TRANSMOGRIFICATION

At TWELVE the Gate of Yin and Yang again appears, beyond which lies the Originating Source itself, represented by the open circle. Above the circle, the Dragon—born from the egg at ELEVEN—flies in every possible space, thus representing the Freedom of Primordial Energy.

LESSON

Return to the Source does not involve an end or extinction, and is not a prize or fantastic goal. It is the final and complete unmasking of the unity of our self-nature and Nature Itself. Nothing need be 'transcended' for nothing can depart from the Primordial Energy of Originating Source. Life should be lived fully on every level since— first and foremost—it's all really Dragon's Play.

Part I

BASIC QUESTIONS ABOUT
THE STAGES OF CULTIVATING THE WAY

So the stages discussed in Part I describe human potential, a path of enlightenment?

We'd rather just say they illustrate the complete terrain of human life. The Stages represent various faces of the fullness of life, not a path *to* something.

But aren't you showing how to get that fruit?

All of us already have the fruit. We're just reviewing what it includes.

How could we already have it?

Our point is—how could we *not* already have it?

Well then, what is it and why do people think that they don't have it?

Our lives, as they are, taken in context, are already in the fruit. When you consider human life out of context, it may seem like the fruit isn't there yet and must somehow be attained.

And what is this context? Also, how do you appreciate that you're in it? Isn't that appreciation something that has to be achieved?

The context is Nature Itself, of course. What else? We are in an incredibly vast, open-ended relationship with Nature, it's already in place. There's nothing we can do about that—we couldn't get out of it if we tried. We might as well look into it more directly and 'exercise' its various aspects. This book simply discusses what they're like.

The way our relationship with Nature is initially perceived, if one wants to talk about how we discover it, is by connecting to *ourselves* as we are. This is not just a preliminary to discovering our relationship to Nature or to discovering Nature, because we are Nature ... we *are* part of it.

So we start with ourselves and open through that. We find the larger world of paths, forests and mountains, and of human society as well. And opening further, we find still more subtle facets of Nature—dynamic factors which ground our lives in profound but unseen ways.

But some characters, like Monkey, seem to be parts of the human psyche.

There are many characters in the story. Monkey is one, so is Sage, but the ground they walk on, the mountain they climb, the sky above them, the Space encompassing that, the luminous view of manifest Nature (NINE), the Immortals who enjoy Nature's openness and manifestations, the Dragon who flies through it—all are significant.

The early characters are facets of "human nature," true, but not necessarily just of a psyche or personality. They are facets of every component of what we are as living creatures, of everything that makes us *alive*. They also illustrate typical ways of relating to our context. And the later characters, like the Immortals and the Dragon, represent facets of our situation—our relationship to Nature—which are truly enormous, fundamental and on-going. They emphasize our full freedom while supporting the options and games of apparent progress typical of ONE through SIX.

We don't achieve the last six Stages—we're saturated by them. We stand on them and are surrounded by them.

So they are not a 'goal' or even an 'accomplishment'?

Right, such Stages are not special attainments and we're not necessarily great yogis when we experience them more directly. They are just part of our situation. For example, the Immortals at TEN and ELEVEN represent the livingness that we all draw upon every second.

"Cultivating the Way" is not "following a path" to some end, although it's quite natural for it to look like that during the early Stages. Most traditional path literature is framed entirely in the "achievement and progress" terms of those Stages. But in Cultivating the full Way, we human beings are not really progressing to the later Stages, we're just celebrating their truth, the fact that they apply to us all. More generally, we shouldn't regard the Stages as features of a map leading to a treasure. In checking our presence in the fruit, we simply visit the Stages and are also visited by them.

Even so, are you talking about discovering Nature, or rather ultimate reality or enlightenment?

Perhaps it doesn't seem like we could be discussing Nature, but that's because people have become accustomed to thinking of Nature as rocks and trees, as somehow 'unenlightened.' But Nature is multidimensional, and our seamless relationship to It actually has many faces—from the claustrophobia and alienation of ONE to the growing friendship through SIX, to the open Space of SEVEN, the harmony of EIGHT, the undiminishable livingness of NINE, TEN, ELEVEN, the freedom of TWELVE.

It's not "ultimate reality," because that implies that there is some other thing, a lesser or illusory place perhaps ... and we're not saying that at all. Monkey and ONE don't represent delusion here, but just a constricted expression of the fullness of the human situation. ONE is still a very potent demonstration of our freedom and fruit.

So you're not documenting the pursuit of some ultimate truth?

No. Again, we're celebrating livingness! Nature and our living connection to It are too vast to be reduced to 'truth,' or to being 'pursued' in any manner. Even emphasizing their 'realization' is a little odd. It's like saying you've 'realized' the Amazon Rain forest—that's very nice, and the early Stages do include that kind of experience. But as the later Stages emphasize, it's even more important that the forest is there, supporting us. So while we seek to participate more deeply and fully in our situation, we do so with humility and a sense of proportion regarding our 'realizations' in the vast and potent context of Nature.

All the early Stages express various aspects of the freedom of Nature and the freedom that Nature gives us, including the option to seem small and cut off, out of context. Like Monkey at ONE, we human beings can make even that radical demonstration of freedom. And it doesn't hurt anything to play that way—it's not 'wrong.'

Whether you look at ONE as ONE or as THIRTEEN is moot ... we're considering ONE as part of Nature's Way that includes TEN, etc., but not really as a preliminary to TEN ... it's just part of a total picture. So ONE is best seen as part of a circle, and thus as THIRTEEN rather than as ONE on a vertical chart of achievement. All the Stages are representative facets of what is encompassed within the same Circle, and they are all in the fruit of our relationship to Nature.

So Nature is both what we are and where we are. And the primacy of this human relationship to Nature is well worth looking into. The old yogic and contemplative traditions essentially performed the service and function of doing just that—exploring and celebrating the full scope of the human relationship to Nature. I.e., wherever they thought they were going, whatever 'enlightenment' they thought they were achieving, they were really, fundamentally, going deeper into some facet of our existing relationship to Nature. They were dramatizing aspects of the operative freedom we all enjoy.

Of course, they phrased their explorations and discoveries in religious or even esoteric terms, and different traditions disagreed about various issues. But whether they would admit it or not, and whatever else you might say they were doing, they were essentially delving into the human relationship to Nature.

And you feel that this view of the ancient yogic traditions matters today, even for lay people in ordinary life?

The exploration of this relationship is just as important now as it ever was. Our concern is not to revive an ancient esoteric sect, but to emphasize the basic issue of the human relationship to Nature. We draw upon the insights of the past only to show more of our situation.

This agenda definitely has relevance to ordinary life in the modern world. It's generally ignored these days, but could be better understood today than it was in the past. The growing appreciation of Earth's global ecology may help illustrate the wider interdependence with Nature which we discuss here. Also, some aspects of the human relationship to Nature don't conform to ordinary common-sense logic, so they seemed 'mystical' thousands of years ago. But some of the recent developments in various branches of medicine and physical science make even unusual dynamic features seem more familiar to us now.

So it's no longer the province of yogic specialists, or of scientists either. Everybody benefits by looking into their place in Nature a little more, respecting and celebrating it.

Cultivating this relationship nourishes us all, individually and collectively—it both taps and feeds into Nature's nourishing capacity. We can thereby consciously partake of it, and also give something back as well.

And this 'cultivation' necessarily begins with Monkey, at ONE?

This cultivation doesn't have a beginning at all—it's happening wherever you find yourself. But our exposition of it starts at ONE. Also, it's a good idea to check your grounding, your experience of the 'lessons' of all the Stages, even if you find yourself 'past' some of them. As for Monkey, he—like the other characters—is not a fixed or specific thing. We can only provide functional, contextual definitions of him ... he's in the body, energy, mind, habits, desires, insights, etc., and is characterized operationally, by his behavior in the individual Stages. In Part II, we look more closely at the complete range of such behavior.

PART 2

COMMENTARIES

We experience ONE when we focus obsessively on *our* lives. ONE is basically an insecure response to life, and leads to claustrophobic isolation and loneliness.

ONE

DISCOVERING MONKEY

At ONE Monkey is alone, perched on the branches of his small tree world, oblivious to the larger field of experience on which his very existence is grounded. His environment is a blur of the frantic activity created by unchecked desire.

Cultivating the Way involves appreciating and expressing our nature in the context of Nature. We can then participate fully in life and in the 'living' environment. Thus, the first issue is to reflect upon ourselves and the context in which we operate.

THE CONSEQUENCES OF A LIMITED APPROACH

At ONE, our appreciation of our nature is quite limited. Our felt connection to the nurturing environment (our context) is thus correspondingly limited. This is the situation of Monkey.

Monkey represents various energetic aspects of our nature, all quite important, but here appearing in a somewhat unruly or rascally guise, apparently acting in isolation. He is 'alone,' perched precariously on branches containing the fruits of desire. He's ungrounded ... oblivious to the tree's trunk or roots, and to the ground in which his tree home grows.

43

Monkey lives in a thick tangle of branches and leaves. He doesn't see the larger world beyond his tree. Even when he tries to survey his surroundings, as shown in the Image, he's really only scanning for intruders while imagining himself King of the Jungle. He's often uncomfortable and frantic in his pursuit of fruit, and is thus unable to appreciate his environment clearly ... it's all just a blur. Monkey lacks the stability and clarity provided by more sustained awareness.

ONE thus represents the unconsidered relationship to Nature, the 'relationship' which posits alienation. Because Monkey lacks any perspective on life, he feels isolated—even relishing his alleged autonomy—and 'relates' to his environment only as food to be plucked and consumed.

EXPERIENCING MONKEY

We can find Monkey by performing a simple experiment. Sit comfortably with a relaxed and unsupported but straight back. Let your hands maintain contact with your knees, palms down. As a preliminary, take three deep breaths and exhale deeply after each one. Your eyes should be open but relaxed, cast downward to a point several feet in front of you. Your lips should remain slightly parted, with the tongue touching the edge of the palette on the roof of the mouth.

Now—breathe in a slow, relaxed manner, with awareness, and count each breath until you reach a count of ten. It sounds easy, doesn't it? In many traditions, an exercise like this would be merely a 'preliminary,' used to "calm the mind" or something of that sort. However, when applied with the view we'll present in this book, which emphasizes experiencing the living continuity that stays with central functions such as breathing, it's an advanced or complete method.

If you try this exercise, you'll probably find that despite your intention to count ten breaths without distraction, you may lose the count entirely or see that other things are going on quite independently of it. In either case, you have encountered Monkey!

At ONE, Monkey is the vital but unruly aspect of ourselves that refuses to remain within the bounds established by some intention or concentration. So while Monkey encompasses all our unbridled potency, at ONE it's usually seen only erratically or indirectly.

The important point to note here is that if you fail to complete the uninterrupted conscious count to ten, and you acknowledge the precise nature of that 'failure,' then you actually *succeed*—you accomplish your purpose, which is *to experience a part of yourself, as you actually are.*

With this experience, you enter into true self reflection. The same point applies if you complete the count, but notice some aspect of yourself that remains outside of the method, busily engaged in other activities.

In fact, this practice can have many possible outcomes—you may, for example, feel that you have *nearly* lost the count but remain "pretty sure" you remember what it was. Or, you may at times easily count to ten because Monkey himself has taken up the task as a game ... this is all still the activity of Monkey.

Thus, Monkey may not particularly chafe at your counting to ten— he may even think it's a lark, or revel in *his* ability to do it ... anything, as long as he himself, as he really is, isn't exposed to the light of awareness. Monkey also likes to raise such distracting questions as "Why bother?," "What is this method for?," "Why not stay asleep or do something more exciting?," etc.

The real issue is not to give Monkey a new game to play, nor to rejoice in succeeding or be concerned about failing. Rather, we should just *see* Monkey. Since Monkey himself squirms around to avoid such revealing perspectives, approaches to meditation which don't understand Monkey are vulnerable to being co-opted by him, extending our stay in ONE.

LIFE AS A "FIX IT" GAME

One of Monkey's favorite ploys is to view meditation as an antidote to some problem you supposedly have—a "fix it" regimen. Monkey encourages us to feel that meditation is supposed to stop our thinking, resolve our confusion, or eliminate conflicting emotions.

Monkey is always pleased by such approaches because he knows that they'll leave him in peace or even give him many entertaining things to do, tussling around high up in the branches ... he'll never have to admit their futility or face participating in the larger and more deeply-grounded issues of the world surrounding his tree.

All "fix it" issues are superficial tangents. The real agenda of cultivating the Way doesn't involve any sort of corrective action, just full participation in our actual situation.

It's unnecessary to struggle with Monkey or try to subdue him—we should simply recognize his presence. When we have the intention to do so, and Monkey breaks that intention, then he has to be acknowledged as an important aspect of our nature.

THE FUTILITY OF "MONKEY FIGHTS"

We can't enlist Monkey in assisting our concentration because he is not yet grounded enough to help. The harder we press in trying to conscript Monkey, the more agitated and erratic he becomes.

If we start feeling angry or judgmental and try to block out or control Monkey, it's really Monkey himself taking over, and his game which keeps us ungrounded. Monkey masquerades as our intention to practice self reflection, then becomes the distractions to that practice, and gets into an hysterical "monkey fight," shrieking and battling with himself. As enraged as he often gets in this process, he still feels quite "at home" in the midst of it. As the Image indicates, this all takes place up in the tree's branches, not on the ground.

The point is not, as some people have claimed, that Monkey is a 'problem' or the source of 'delusion' and deliberately seeks to deceive. It's simply his nature to want to *do* things, often quite unpredictably and without regard for the rest of our nature or Nature. Also, it's painful for him to face the fact that his assertions of independence do not, after

all, make him powerful. He overreacts to the imposition of larger perspectives, but cannot avoid sensing that there is something missing.

*(Monkey's) erratic movements, full of uneasiness and paranoia,
leave him breathless. In this limited fantasy world he is sometimes
clever and amusing, but his overall experience of life is
claustrophobic.*

To summarize, Monkey is animated by irrepressible energy and desire.
He's obsessed with asserting potency, with getting and guarding his
fruit. He thinks this fruit will last forever, and that his clever and
skillful cavorting and his aggressive behavior will keep other monkeys away—"it's all rightly his!" He feels free and dominant in this
conduct, but again, because he lacks a solid ground and a large perspective, he can't fully accept his own conclusions or assess his situation. His is really a very small and unsteady kingdom.

As we begin to recognize Monkey, we also experience the suffocat-
ing and claustrophobic quality of a life characterized by energy operating without *apparent* connection to its complete context. Once we
feel and acknowledge the frustration of this approach, we have to
consider "coming down from the isolation of the tree." Thus, even
the simple exercise in self-reflection and concentration we've just discussed can have a profound effect on our lives.

THE BASIC ISSUE AT ONE

First we must see the limitations of Monkey's situation while sus-
pending judgment (avoiding over-reactions and hysteria). We thus
gently reflect on the dynamics of Monkey's activity, but remain concentrated. So, we can count ten breaths in a calm state which is still
broad and realistic, while allowing Monkey his own special characteristics. This is the advent of TWO.

TWO is like a freeze-frame image of our natural urge to self-reflect. However, here this urge is still laden with doubt and reluctance.

TWO

MONKEY MEETS SAGE

At TWO Monkey comes face to face with Sage. Sage is another vantage point within a new and enlarged environment.

Sage is shown as a Confucian gentleman-scholar, very properly attired, with his hands in his sleeves. His name is not intended to suggest that he possesses extraordinary wisdom and insight. In ancient China, the Confucian 'sage' was basically a very learned, disciplined, and rather idealistic person who strove to be impeccable in his behavior and of service to society. For Sage, "impeccable behavior" means "correct etiquette" and he has studied etiquette carefully.

'Sage' represents the rather channeled aspects of our being which, in the early stages of the Way, might appear to include a focussed or continuous awareness, perhaps even a 'conscience,' etc. This is not to say that Monkey doesn't also involve awareness, but just that his acknowledgment of being connected with Nature emphasizes satisfying the appetites of the moment, unconsidered and direct responses. Sage's appreciation of his nature and connection to Nature is characterized more by self reflection and heartfelt, even dutiful concerns.

Sage considers overviews and issues that go beyond the appetites of the moment. He has perspectives related to cultural attitudes and belief systems that bear upon one's character and conscience, and portray "our position and responsibility in the universe," etc. In that sense, his self-reflection is heavily conditioned, socialized and shaped by education, full of notions about propriety, codes of conduct, and long-range, idealistic agendas.

THE EMERGENCE OF THE SAGE

Our Sagely aspects can undertake regimens and aspire to goals that go beyond temporary personal gratification. Hence, we are capable of concentration and discipline, even of sustained feeling or sentiment. When we can count ten breaths without being completely taken over by Monkey, then Sage has begun to clearly emerge.

Monkey may certainly still *appear* without blocking TWO (as long as he doesn't actually break the count). At TWO, Monkey doesn't contribute to the count's continuity, but for a little while at least, he doesn't obscure Sage's solid presence and steady activity. The appreciation of this transition from ONE to TWO can occur in the blink of an eye.

Sage is not really new, in the sense of being something just created and still in his infancy—he is shown fully mature. He isn't at all a stranger to us, but does stand in greater relief as a result of our exercise in self-reflection and concentration.

A DUAL VIEW

Duality is the major theme here. Monkey's speed and heedlessness at ONE simply didn't permit him to appreciate the many features, dualisms, and contradictions already inherent in that situation. For example, his realm seemed very big to him, but was really quite small. With TWO, therefore, comes a second vantage point and the enlarged sense of *context* needed for us to notice such contrasts.

In TWO, Monkey and Sage are not fighting, but just existing. The Sage is not going anywhere, and has no particular intention yet. He simply sees Monkey, and recognizes his own 'grounded' existence by contrasting himself with Monkey, who is still hanging and swinging wildly about in his tree while he eyes Sage.

No major reality shift has occurred. Neither character quite knows what to make of the other, and so neither is moved to change his own point of view or preferences.

At this stage, particularly as you count up to thirty breaths, with concentration, you have found a true state of focussed presence to which you can easily return. TWO is thus more stable and inclusive than ONE, but is still limited in being a kind of 'standoff' between two entrenched perspectives.

> *The two figures, however, are 'frozen' in the duality of mutual self-discovery. They primarily dwell upon comparisons and labeling. Monkey views Sage as idealistic and impractical. Sage views Monkey as selfish and unprincipled.*

This condition of an alert 'standoff' continues until you can count at least thirty breaths (the entry into THREE). Until then, Monkey and Sage remain quite separate but locked in patterns of comparisons ... so you alternate from one view to the other.

"This Sage character is really an odd duck, so stiff and stuck up. Where are his hands and feet? Does he ever move? I'll bet he can't even walk, much less swing and leap like I can! He looks so caught up in his visions and ideals ... he has no spontaneity, no ability to live in the present! He does seem steady and calm though ... I wonder why ... what's going on down there?"

"This Monkey has possibilities, but he's such a barbarian! No manners, no respect for others, no thoughts for the future, lost in an hysterical frenzy of lewd showing off. Still, it's all rather poignant, in a way ... the innocent savage. It all reminds me of that poem I read last year ... but I had no idea monkeys were so quick and strong!"

DIFFERENCES AND DOMINANCE

In ONE, we identified with Monkey to survive, because he appeared to be the strong one, the one who got things done. He also seemed free to act as he chose. Since he was alone and his way of life could not be compared with others, he also seemed less wild or reckless. Now, the presence of Sage casts Monkey in a new light and raises serious questions about Monkey's primacy. But we can't really say that one is free or capable and the other isn't ... rather, the important questions become "What am I?," "Where am I?," "What's going on?"

Attempted answers to such questions reflect the differences between Monkey and Sage. One is materialistic, the other idealistic or religious, one is unabashedly self-serving while the other has a social conscience and may even be altruistic, one is nervous and unpredictable, the other calm and solid, etc.

At TWO, we see ourselves in terms of these rigid dichotomies. We're also 'frozen' in alternating modes of action.

When we're interacting in the busy-body world of everyday affairs, we become Monkey, taking advantage of his "can do" energy. On the other hand, self reflection remains limited to a special time, a special state. Sage is stuck on the meditation cushion, insistent on regimens such as counting breath with correct posture, etc. He can't operate *freely* in the world at large.

It's true that Sage is already on the ground, while Monkey is still lost in his own private fantasy world, but Sage's ground is only a little patch at TWO, and no real path has appeared yet. Sage is quite stuck there. Thus, his ground doesn't look any bigger or more promising than does Monkey's tree ... both are small, isolated, and so Monkey and Sage still doubt each other's significance.

This doubt, however, also extends to their original perceptions of *themselves*. Now their doubt forces them to take each other seriously enough to be willing to take turns ... on a very tentative, distrustful "trial basis."

ALTERNATING APPROACHES TO LIFE

So, while ONE was a kind of insanity, where our life force is being driven and drained heedlessly, TWO is a more sane state in which there are two approaches: we can be energetic and wild in a limited context of freedom which permits some movement and change, and we can also be strong and stable in another, 'recuperative' awareness of freedom within a more fixed context.

There's still considerable hesitation and doubt, and some mutual disdain and mockery, between Monkey and Sage. Yet each has his time. This situation is not particularly profound or creative, but it's healthier than ONE.

A NOTE ON HEALTH IN CULTIVATING THE WAY

The issue of 'health' is only subtly furthered by the tentative addition of a new perspective in TWO, but will acquire a general and growing relevance in the ensuing Stages of Cultivating the Way. Again, the main point throughout will be the human relationship to Nature, to participate fully in our nature and to express its connection to Nature.

This both requires and defines 'health'—health is a balanced, sensitive, and complete interaction between the various facets of our existence and our environment. The natural connection or unity of all these factors should be experienced … otherwise, health is lost and so are the sensitivity and vitality involved in Cultivating the Way.

The purpose of health, therefore, is not to support personal longevity in some narrow, self-serving sense. Health permits a full, open-ended participation in the illuminating processes of the living universe.

At ONE, we enjoy the potency of Monkey but lack any appreciation of the fundamental ground of life. In TWO, Sage is in touch with the ground, but cannot move freely on it, as Monkey could if he were so inclined. Sage just "knows more about it"—he's sufficiently focussed and educated to understand and respect it in a general way. He's a good—though limited—trustee of life, but no more than that. He isn't sensitive to our organism's particular, time-specific needs.

Monkey, meanwhile, uses his awareness of basic biological cycles only to motivate all sorts of compulsive behavior … to sate poorly-understood desires. He's sensitive in a strictly selective way, and constantly over-reacts to physical urges rather than seeking understanding and a healthy measure in life.

However, as the Way opens further and the natural balance of our existence becomes more evident, health will be easily sustained and will in turn grow in scope to reflect the splendid character of Nature and the human situation … a celebration of life founded in the uneasy doubts of TWO.

BALANCE

Balance is not an issue for Monkey because he continues to deny some fundamental realities associated with his needs and with the larger environment ranging out from the ground beneath his tree. "Only my tree's branches are real, and they don't need any 'ground'! The entire world is already within reach!"

Monkey convinced us in ONE that we basically consist of grasping, desire-oriented tendencies, unconnected with any more stable, enduring 'ground' qualities of existence. He hasn't yet relinquished that view to reveal himself and his connections with our ground and with Nature.

Sage has some definite sense of the ground's importance. But he's rooted to a small patch of it in a way that obscures its true extent ... his nature is still polarized to appear rigidly conservative as a response to Monkey's seemingly radical activity. His appreciation of Monkey's vitality is starting to develop, but has hardly become more than a fascination with Monkey's antics up in the branches.

In general, the discovery of our multifaceted nature is important, but shouldn't cause us to become stuck in either Monkey-Sage comparisons or alternating Monkey-Sage perceptions and actions. Neither Monkey nor Sage are in a position, acting separately and in separate spheres, to live very effectively.

But all this judgment and labeling produce no real advantage.

It's important that we see through the dualisms and alternations of Monkey and Sage. However, this doesn't mean that we should try to eliminate dualism by taking sides and rejecting one in favor of the other ... that would just be giving reign to judgments again.

Most contemplative traditions seek to transcend TWO's dualism by taming Monkey, subjecting him to the will of Sage. Taoism, on the other hand, respects Monkey and does not recommend trying to reform or discipline him at all ... he plays a vital role in the cultivation

55

of the Way, without *ever* being changed or subjugated. This is a simple matter of sanity in viewing the many faces of life's energy.

We don't need to fix our natures, or to battle the apparent dualisms within us. Sage does not need a 'leash' to restrain or control Monkey. Extending the influence of Sage and suppressing Monkey isn't desirable, or even possible, in the long run.

We must learn to see duality's operation as an essential part of what's real, and as suggestive of the dynamics and rich possibilities of life. This relaxed tolerance naturally gives rise to THREE.

THREE is a more trusting approach to life, allowing us to act from intuition and instinct.

THREE

JOURNEYING TOGETHER

At THREE Monkey leaves the confines of his tree world as he and Sage agree to begin a journey together. They turn their backs on the fruitless judgments of TWO, and venture forward in their new and expanding environment.

At TWO, Monkey was still determined to cling to his branches and stick to his fruit diet, being particularly partial to the fruits that grow high on the tops of trees. He was also convinced, without adequate direct experience, that the ground was dull, irrelevant or perhaps even dangerous—if there was anything living down there at all, it was probably something that ate monkeys!

Of course, Monkey never actually *checked* the ground himself. "Why bother? All the action is up in the tree, isn't it?"

Seeing the Sage standing calmly and determinedly below him has challenged many of Monkey's preconceptions and also stimulated his greed ... the self-doubt of TWO has had its effect. Monkey is perfectly equipped to walk on the ground, and now he has a reason to do so—the expectation of huge fruits and new tree tops to rule somewhere. "That Sage may be onto something big!" So Monkey descends ...

REALISM

It's important to see and accept Monkey's real desires, and not pretend that he would be content to give up his tree here for something intangible. At any given Stage, we can really only have the motives appropriate to that Stage, and it's pointless to cover them up or overlay them with more 'correct' or noble intentions founded in pretense. This too is important to being on the Way.

If we refuse to acknowledge and respect Monkey's characteristics, and foolishly develop a meditative skill around or in spite of them, we're eliminating part of the real fruit of cultivation and we're also running a risk. If, for example, we somehow succeeded in carrying such an uneven development into a deep state of contemplation, Monkey might surface unexpectedly and quickly draw us into more than we can handle.

It's best to appreciate and work *with* Monkey, from the outset. This is the significance of THREE. Monkey has come down out of his tree, and Sage accepts his company. Monkey effectively undertakes to be Sage's disciple (at least until he finds the 'superfruit'!), and Sage agrees to give Monkey the benefit of his experience and vision so they may forge ahead.

VIEWS AND MOTIVES

With his greed intact, Monkey has decided that he'll gain by going somewhere with Sage. Sage is freed from being stuck to his spot by realizing that he *can* travel once he enters into a relationship with Monkey.

One of the reasons Sage was stuck until this point is that he was actually afraid of moving. He was brave enough on his own special spot, but lacked the confidence to vary his situation. Now he feels ready to break through his limiting conditions. Because, he sees Monkey's vitality and skillfulness, and believes Monkey will be able to help him deal with difficult situations, to leap over obstacles.

Of course, Sage's view is a little simplistic here—"With Monkey's power and flexibility clearing the way for me, I'll be able to move through the world without being disturbed!"

Sage also thinks he can transform Monkey into a gentleman, and is naively confident in his sense of superiority and self-righteousness, inspired in part by the fact that Monkey *came down to him,* rather than the reverse. (He tends to ignore Monkey's real motives.)

This is the stage at which people often see cultivation in a religious or moral light, because it still has a moral ground (represented by the Confucian sage), and even a moral mission—the transformation or rectification of Monkey. However, like the Taoist cultivators of old, we recommend putting these tendencies and events in a more neutral perspective, recognizing that Sage and Monkey are simply behaving according to their natures.

Sage may *try,* for a while, to reform Monkey—that's entirely natural—but this reformation is not the central issue, and it's vital to begin considering that. Sage and Monkey are equal in importance and incapable of being fundamentally changed or improved.

TOLERANCE AND TRUST

The main point of THREE is the development of *tolerance.* Monkey and Sage are finally both on the ground, working together, and this facilitates a much more integrated approach to daily life. So even if you continue to operate using only one of these two vantage points for quite a while, there's no conflict.

When Sage advises Monkey to be patient or to go in a certain direction which produces no immediate discoveries, Monkey tolerates this because he thinks Sage knows something. And when Monkey finally gets restless and says "Look at these new trees ... I'm going to stop and collect all that fruit!" Sage just sits down and waits while Monkey follows his nature.

They're not only developing tolerance, but trust as well. They accommodate each other without fear of jeopardizing their own objectives.

The arising of tolerance and trust between various aspects of our nature is essential to Embarking on the Way. Indeed, this emphasis on an on-going and ever-extending *relationship* has always been the main point of Taoism, and remains as vital as ever for everyone.

Of course, the characters of Monkey and Sage are still quite different. Sage, for all his self-righteous reserve, doesn't really know what's going on! He continues to think of cultivation in quietist terms, as being a state of equanimity. Monkey is still pushing Sage around, eager to find better fruit. But because they're working together now, their concentration can become bigger, more flexible, and more sensitive to their environment.

ON THE VERGE

Standing and operating in the same sphere at THREE, their environment is appreciated slightly for the first time, since now they can help each other focus on it and explore it a bit. They have more space to breathe and consider their situation. But they still lack a sense of what to do or where to go. This is indicated in the Image by the fact that they're facing away, looking into an unknown territory. Three's budding cooperative relationships are still largely internal affairs, so its relationship to Nature "at large" is one characterized by uncertainty.

As the Image shows, they've turned their backs on the confusing entanglements of ONE. They're very close to a new understanding— they only need each other and the ground beneath their feet.

Also at THREE, the ground becomes a more prominent aspect of the picture, representing the growing depth and solidity of Monkey and Sage's relationship. This emerging ground is the basis of their journey.

The mutual acceptance which grows between Monkey and Sage results from their sharing the same ground, and in turn helps them acknowledge and cooperatively use that ground. The ground is the essential overlap in Monkey and Sage, so as they come to "pull together," they're also returning to the most central, common aspects

A NOTE ON MONKEY, SAGE, AND GROUND

The story of Monkey, Sage, and the ground of their relationship has a significance that includes many levels of meaning and areas of application. But like life, it could never be reduced to a single set of such applications, however large that set might be. It's more important to take the story on its own terms, appreciating its basic trends and issues, than to restrict attention to one or more particular interpretations of the characters (Monkey, Sage, etc).

It is, of course, useful to see how the characters relate to various facets of human nature. For example, you might find Monkey and Sage to correspond well to your energy and focussed awareness, respectively, both 'meeting' in the body, where the 'ground' of life becomes more apparent. They might also both be found within your energy itself, as well as within your awareness, physical functioning, etc.

In general, Monkey is the essence of vitality, unfettered but willing to enliven structures and discipline … he's the potency to reach out to the universe. Sage personifies regularity, steadiness and sustained presence, patterns and an acceptance of limits. When they're taken together, the ground of their relationship is seen to be open-ended and balanced, permitting still more experience of the human relationship to Nature.

Someone concentrating on the conduct of ordinary life might discover these characters in the simplest and most familiar of attitudes and personal qualities. In the process, "ordinary life" would be illuminated. And if you were to engage in the practice of technical yogic methods, you might also recognize Monkey and Sage in more subtle forms and at subtle levels. Monkey is then akin to the energy which—when seen within the context of the yogic channels (the Sage patterning)—is regulated and inspires our appreciation of the fullness of life. Monkey's erratic or 'renegade' character even reflects the open, chaotic dimension of Nature Itself, while Sage represents Nature's fundamental 'conventions' (see the discussion of SEVEN and EIGHT).

All such discoveries are based on a growing breadth and flexibility in our experience of the 'ground' of humanness.

of their own true natures. The ground may thus also be considered as the fundamental field or atmosphere which encompasses their existence, and is therefore not really separable from the entire fabric and extent of Nature Itself.

As one facet of the ground of our existence in Nature, the body is more explicitly a part of our experience at THREE. Cultivating the Way has now both broadened and "descended to the body," so it includes the physicality of life and Nature. This is becoming evident even in simple exercises like the counting of breath.

While you practice that exercise, especially as the count extends naturally from thirty to one-hundred-and-eight, Monkey is actually contributing to it. Monkey adds energy and an expanded, more flexible and multifaceted sense of continuity to the steadiness of Sage. This is a matter of finding continuity *where and as it's actually happening,* rather than clinging to Sage's initially restricted and idealized notions of it.

Since the body is now more involved in the exercise, you may experience back pains, nervous twitches, numbness in the legs, etc. These tend to seem irrelevant or distracting, but again, taking our cue from Taoism, they should be seen as aspects of the body's growing participation, which must, like Monkey, be appreciated more completely and included, rather than being filtered out, pacified, or 'fixed.' The body is much more than just a necessary evil or a mere 'basis' for cultivation. The same point can be made for all other facets of the 'ground.'

Just as Monkey and Sage must stand and walk on the ground together, we must live, interact, and explore the world through our totality. So, as we attend more directly to the full ground of our existence, and come to see the possibilities it offers for linking us to the rest of Nature, FOUR unfolds.

At FOUR, self-respect, acceptance, and confidence become more prominent. These qualities are reflected in the formation of cooperative relationships with others, and also permit us an inkling of 'fate.'

FOUR

EMBARKING ON THE WAY

At FOUR Monkey and Sage come upon a Path that cuts through a rich and varied new environment.

The Image of FOUR shows much more of the ground beneath Monkey's tree. Monkey, Sage, and ground are now equally prominent.

The experimental tolerance and mutual acceptance of the previous stages have now brought this new factor into play. Moreover, the ground is seen clearly for the first time—it's actually *a path.*

Monkey and Sage are both surprised to discover a clear path. In THREE, Sage still doubted that his association with Monkey was going to accomplish anything, and Monkey was entirely unfamiliar with paths... he'd been thinking of his future with Sage in quite different terms. Suddenly, a highway opens up in front of them.

This is the first time they "find something together." It's very much a mutual discovery, causing shock and glee in both of them—"Hey, look at this!" Previously, their mutual acceptance was based on a strategy of "I'm in my world, you're in yours," or "I'll play along with you for a little while." But now they find that their tolerance has exposed a new world or dimension, well worth exploring as a team.

The natural cooperation between various facets of our existence effortlessly reveals the ground of the fullness of life. Through the sensitivity of our integrated nature, we discover that this ground includes a wondrous, open-ended environment or context for living creatively. It's essentially a matter of 'walking,' vigorously engaging ourselves, and thereby coming upon a 'road' permitting full access to Nature. The path is simply following the Way of our own nature.

Since there is now a clear and relevant path, we're not drifting or listless. FOUR is therefore the basis for a growing natural intention or motive to cultivate the Way.

> *They sense that their journey now contains elements of a destiny, and their confidence grows. They also feel what they must do. This new environment stimulates many insights that clarify their intentions.*

The Monkey and Sage, now well-grounded and cooperating, both contribute to a deep and continuous concentration, and therefore to a much keener view. Many truly helpful and important insights are thus readily available at FOUR, and should be actively sought, enjoyed, and used. However, amplified perceptions and the accumulation of knowledge are not ends in themselves.

REASSURANCES AND RISKS

Four offers an interesting and varied path through the forest of life, and part of the path's value is the opportunity it provides to exercise ourselves and to learn *what and where we are* from that exercise. Monkey and Sage have both left their original turfs to travel together, and that opens them up to an appreciation of "being in the world." But this path hasn't yet yielded a sufficiently panoramic view to provide a clear sight of what lies ahead. We must therefore avoid chasing new sensations at the cost of abandoning the path itself.

Perceptions are so rich and information-laden here (to an unaccustomed degree) that we run the risk of getting lost in side trips. That could ultimately result in our forgetting our integration and becoming less sensitive again, or in failing to use our connection to the ground of life in a fully creative and beneficial way.

Of course, it's tremendously exhilarating and reassuring to get so much feedback—becoming connected to a nurturing and meaningful environment or context for action proves that we're not alone in an uncaring or inaccessible universe. But along with this perception of one's self and the resulting heightened knowledge of our environment, we need true self-respect without self-cherishing or self-importance. Otherwise, our new discoveries would lack significance

SELF-RESPECT

Self-respect consists partly in staying in touch with the integration bonding all our various facets (such as body, energy, awareness, etc.), rather than selling it out for knowledge or taking it as the justification for feelings of self-importance. Thus, the key 'knowledge' in FOUR is an appreciation of *integration itself,* without overly emphasizing the information or potency received through that integration.

The other main component of self-respect is the understanding that this integration must be used or exercised, in order to be understood and extended. At FOUR, although Monkey and Sage often have droll notions about their ultimate objectives, they're periodically "brought back to earth" by their *active* engagement with the path.

They can now glimpse the central point that even the 'goal' itself is simply following the way of their natures. They'll thus travel together in an increasingly grounded and open interaction with Nature. Stages beyond FOUR are merely an elaboration of what that insight, still incomplete at FOUR, really involves.

However, despite their continued cooperation, their apparent uniqueness and individuality are not yet diminished. Sage, still full of spiritual idealism, prepares himself for a noble commitment to a great Quest. Monkey, as hungry as ever, imagines great epicurean delights at the end of their journey.

Chinese literature contains many stories about a monkey and sage, often portraying a friendship between them which is, at times, both comical and adversarial. These tales represent various aspects of FOUR's possibilities.

SAGE'S VIEW

Sage retains his Confucian character, so he sees FOUR as the revelation of his destiny as a would-be exemplar. There's a bit of the Confucian in all of us, urging us on to serve as righteous models for the world. We seek and find an ideal, something to be, and then consider that we have both a right and a duty to embody that.

Once this Confucian Sage arrives at FOUR, his yearnings and idealistic searching suddenly seem validated. So while Monkey is running wild with excitement at this stage, Sage becomes even more firmly composed, settling into a stone-like commitment to the path.

Sage's commitment now includes the intention to preserve his relationship with Monkey, because it was through this association that FOUR was discovered. Moreover, Sage fears that the newly-exposed path may become steep or involve trials and obstacles which could cause him to lose his deportment. "Monkey, with his ferocity and vitality, might continue to prove useful."

Although the path responds to Sage's deepest yearnings, close inspection shows him that it isn't at all tame or civilized. Sage begins to appreciate, vaguely, that Monkey's wildness is itself a part of the emerging path, *a proper and necessary characteristic of the path's living dimension,* which can't be avoided or left behind.

MONKEY'S VIEW

Monkey is equally confirmed in his desire to continue with this adventure. The new fruits of his relationship with Sage are spectacular, and make him begin to forget his own small tree. He sees that the larger environment of the forest and surrounding world is real, likely to offer rich rewards. Sage's emphasis on heavenly pursuits is also starting to rub off on Monkey, so he imagines a kind of heavenly fruit, which would satisfy his hunger for lifetimes, perhaps even make him immortal!

Monkey is quivering and frantic in the face of so many possibilities. Left to himself, he could easily lose the path in pursuit of various fruits. Sage, however, knows that the function of paths is to go somewhere, and is determined not to be diverted now that he's finally found his Way.

Since Monkey cannot subvert Sage, and prefers not to abandon him (thereby losing the benefit of Sage's knowledge), he ensures that Sage doesn't become rooted to some point along the path, lost in idealistic reveries and intimidated by the prospects of hazards ahead. He pulls Sage along in the only direction left to them—forward, into regions they both hope for and fear.

BALANCE

Acting from a new-found spiritual sanity and maturity, we don't attempt to coddle Monkey and Sage by isolating ourselves from the rigors of life. Nor do we try to repress or eliminate the characteristics unique to Monkey and Sage.

FOUR is characterized by natural balance and discipline, which keep Monkey and Sage on the path, traveling as an expression of their relationship. This discipline is not something Sage has but Monkey lacks—it's inherent in the ground of their relationship itself, and embraces their distinct motives.

The relationship between Monkey, Sage, and ground is the touchstone for all further progress. Methods such as the "breath counting" technique used in the previous stages are no longer necessary. Cultivation can now be based entirely on following the clear path presented by one's diverse but integrated nature, and on the latter's more pronounced connection to Nature.

This is not to say that an awareness of breathing itself is now unnecessary, for breathing is a classic example of a primary process which links all aspects of ourselves and emphasizes our interaction with Nature. The point is rather that the techniques of FIVE and the more subtle and profound activities characteristic of the later Stages become available to us because we've begun to appreciate and to live *instinctively* in the awareness of such basic natural processes.

CHALLENGES OF A RISING GROUND

The Way described so far (ONE through FOUR) is distinguished primarily by its *inclusiveness*. It emphasizes taking our various components along with us rather than trying to abandon, deactivate, or change them.

However, this Way is about to diverge still more sharply from other approaches to cultivation, as the 'landscape' or terrain of our nature rises up like a mountain in the Image of FIVE. Techniques will then necessarily be chosen based on the practicalities of optimizing each person's unique nature and relationship to the environment. This concreteness and precision is critical for the safe, beneficial exploration of FIVE.

At FIVE, an active appetite for life awakens. It's an "eye on the goal" experience. Discriminating intelligence and personal discipline also become operative, rendering us attentive students of our situations in life.

FIVE

REACHING THE MOUNTAIN

*At FIVE Sage and Monkey find themselves on higher ground, with
a broad view to the distant mountains. The central peak, promising
a still larger vista, becomes their goal.*

At the beginning of FIVE, Monkey and Sage pause, reflecting on
what they've experienced so far and considering their new situation.
They're both asking "What did I want? Is this it?," and "Where are
we going?"

Such questions are inevitable, but quickly answered. For, their path
now leads out across a forest and, rising up precipitously, disappears
into various chasms among the huge mountains ahead, finally reap-
pearing leading up the highest peak. They see no path back down,
and conclude that this peak itself must be the goal.

FIVE is thus shaped to some extent by a maturation of insight arising from the mutual acceptance of THREE and the knowledge of
FOUR. This broader view enables Monkey and Sage to see, from afar,
the end of their path.

THE NEW AGENDA

After reviewing their journey and taking stock of the scene before
them, they direct their actions toward the completion appropriate

to their natures. The ascent involves many unknowns, but the bond between them is now reassuringly strong.

Their abilities and relationship are about to be tested as never before. The scope of the mountain range before them represents a stability, diversity, and encompassing touchstone for sanity which they must make their own. Also, the importance of physical stamina as the basis for a practical, concrete spirituality is now apparent.

Monkey and Sage are humbled by the scene and its implications. But they are also, in their respective ways, inspired to go forward.

> *Now that the goal seems clear, they feel greatly inspired and strengthened. However, the path at their feet splits into countless trails leading through vast expanses of uncharted territory.*

Their path has led them to what Sage has feared all along: difficult, varied, and complex terrain. Through FOUR, Sage continued to cling to the image of the "straight and narrow," a self-righteous, duty- and discipline-oriented tradition that is nice and flat, well-defined, even universal.

Sage is now rather concerned that things have gotten rough and ragged, that he may have to roll up his sleeves and extend himself, or even get down on all fours to traverse the ground ... an incredible prospect! He dreads being degraded or embarrassed.

On the other hand, Sage is also deeply moved by the view of the commanding peak ahead. This new image reinforces his long-cherished belief that righteousness—based on the highest and most correct view—dominates Nature. From the peak, Sage knows he would act with authority and correctness.

Monkey, meanwhile, sees the mountain as a big tree without branches ... basically, it's just something to climb. Moreover, he spies a tree line part way up the mountain ridge, and is confident of finding wondrous fruit there. He imagines the peak as the ideal territory to possess and defend. Of course, the mountain also holds many terrors for Monkey, but Sage's obvious resolve and undoubted knowledge support his own willingness to strike onward.

FIVE'S MAZE OF POSSIBILITIES

The cultivator of the Way is now more of an 'everyman', experiencing fairly universal versions of the challenges presented by the human relationship to Nature. So cultivation now echoes the findings of great yogis and religious or social thinkers of the past.

FIVE is thus the place that presents us with a myriad alternative paths of ascent, with all the traditional meditation techniques, philosophies, and codes of behavior competing for our attention. In order to keep our cultivation effective here, we must avoid launching into a binge of spiritual consumerism, mistaking traditions and methods for the goal.

Essentially, FIVE is the Stage of spiritual technology, 'practices,' and as such is quite familiar to people in many traditions. We cannot even begin to treat it in any detail, for the literature and information associated with it is enormous, and actually constitutes the bulk of what some traditions discuss. Our goal is simply to put FIVE in its proper context. For, people frequently get lost here. There is a great temptation to think that the entire Way happens at FIVE and requires the technical skills or powers that people often find so seductive.

FIVE has its place, but is only a small part of Cultivating the Way. It should be explored with vigor but also with discrimination and even a certain degree of reluctance. For, precisely because people often try stretching FIVE to encompass the entire Way, many of the practices attempted at FIVE are really just mimicry of natural activities properly founded in the later Stages, and should not be taken up as 'techniques' here. What occurs spontaneously at EIGHT or TEN may be a waste of time or even dangerous to try at FIVE, due to the rather narrow sense of cultivation that still prevails.

In some instances, traditional maps and even rather complex or antique methods may indeed be appropriate at FIVE, but we must use them strictly like tools, with awareness. All idealisms and attachments to exotica must be put aside in favor of realism.

In such situations, Sage likes to rely on the "tried and true," the maps provided by authorities of the past, while Monkey is both ready and willing to take short cuts. Which of these approaches is correct depends on the individual case, and requires proper functioning of the Monkey-Sage relationship to discover and monitor.

INTEGRATED INTELLIGENCE

Success depends precisely on the sensitivity and responsiveness afforded by this cooperative bond between Monkey and Sage. Without it, the ascent of FIVE would be difficult or impossible to complete safely.

This is why Taoism recommends cultivating this relationship from the outset, beginning at TWO, as a central aspect of 'spiritual' life. Attempting to develop such an effective partnership starting at FIVE— while faced with FIVE's rigors and immediate dangers, demanding mutual trust and well-practiced coordinated 'teamwork'—is a common and serious strategic error.

If an accommodation between Monkey and Sage is begun at TWO, and refined by THREE and FOUR, then by FIVE Monkey and Sage will have entered into a well-tested and affectionate relationship. They not only realize that they can be useful to each other, but they're actually like brothers.

So, although Monkey is eager to take short cuts, he's also very careful now not to strand Sage somewhere. He assesses his choice of route to ensure that Sage will be able to follow along with him. Similarly, Sage wants to make sure that Monkey doesn't get into trouble by moving too quickly or by taking inappropriate risks. Sage's ability to anticipate now includes a fairly broad understanding of what excites or triggers Monkey's reactions, and of the outcome of these spontaneous responses.

The intelligence required at FIVE thus derives from the increasing overlap exposed by integration, from the quintessential character shared by both Monkey and Sage. Sage is still focussed, disciplined, and dutiful, but his acceptance of Monkey has made him less rigid, more interactive. So his sense of discipline is no longer inflexible or maintained with effort. Similarly, Monkey's frantic craziness has the seed of an unique, 'nonlinear,' adaptive intelligence that is fully activated and rendered usable by his cooperation with Sage.

Monkey contributes vital, responsive action and Sage contributes knowledge, steadiness, and a natural, self-regulating discipline. The partnership generates a true intelligence through which we can select and use the right type of activity (meditation, yoga, etc.) to continue our ascent. This empowers us to accept and meet FIVE's challenge.

THE CONCRETE APPROACH TO LIFE

This challenge is very far-reaching. Climbing a mountain is not sitting passively on a meditation cushion. We must allow our practice of meditative methods, the conduct of daily life—and indeed, *all* our experiences and activities—to become linked. 'Meditation' and 'yoga' are thus greatly enlarged, ceasing to apply merely to techniques or special states of awareness.

FIVE is a strenuous engagement in life, interacting with the environment through our physically-based and thoroughly-integrated experience. The ability to respond sensitively to particular situations emphasizes having a more fully-vitalized sense of presence. This is why, in FIVE, our integrated nature comes to loom large, like the Mountain.

As one of the many facets of the unifying 'ground' and concrete presence of human existence, the body itself is now experienced in a much more direct *and visceral* way. At FIVE, we appreciate the body in its plain but also very sophisticated functioning ... it's not asleep, overlaid with fantasies, or only selectively felt. Monkey and Sage now connect with and traverse its full extent, noting its reactions and addressing its specific needs.

Of course, they do this for strictly strategic reasons—they still see this accommodation as a means to an end (achieving the peak). But looking ahead to SIX and beyond, such accommodation of our multifaceted nature itself will become the 'end,' the real fruit of their effort. For now, it's sufficient to note that the Way includes an inherently physical dimension, where the term 'physical' is understood to have a very broad and open-ended application.

LIMITED VIEWS OF PHYSICAL INTELLIGENCE

The approach we're recommending is quite distinct from 'spiritual' traditions which ignore or repress the body. But it also differs from martial and yogic traditions (even those deriving from some Taoist lineages) which make a goal of physical culture or of FIVE itself (viewed simply as 'mountaineering').

Cultivating the Way is really not 'meditative athleticism.' But some traditions nevertheless construe it as such, and thus often use practices which are predominantly physical (in the most ordinary and limited sense) from the beginning. It's a long path to arrive at FIVE's landscape using only the efforts, strength, and skill of the 'muscular' body rather than the natural responses of the actual, quite 'visceral' body. Continuing on in the former way to FIVE's summit would be even more difficult, because FIVE's rigors place a premium on a broadly-functioning intelligence which can tell us how to live through our bodies and energy in a wide variety of circumstances.

To consider Cultivating the Way as just mountaineering is extremely common, and appeals to peoples' desire for romantic or heroic adventures. But it's a very small view, with limited potency.

The mountain is not just an ascending trail—it's huge, beyond any heroic imaginings of the Monkey and Sage prior to FIVE. This makes the classic Taoist point that our emerging visceral, energetic, and sensitive, attentive nature is far more intelligent and properly directed than a mere mind or ego. Even our action in something as 'simple' as digesting lunch requires more intelligence—and also celebrates our relationship to Nature better in some respects—than does applying some complex 'spiritual' technique with our minds alone.

The important points of cultivation are already *in* our full, integrated nature, and don't need to be added, invented, or learned elsewhere. Monkey and Sage must necessarily come to terms with that, clambering around over the extent of the Mountain so they may thoroughly connect with its intelligence.

Again, the objective of FIVE's exercises is not physical culture or training but experiencing how our complete organism actually works. It's not a matter of conquering the Mountain or of spending a lifetime getting strong or sophisticated while exploring it, but of simply getting acquainted with it.

PANORAMIC VISION

As has been true in the previous stages, part of the real point of FIVE is simply the continuity of practice, exercising the intelligence of our integrated nature. However, in the case of FIVE, this exercise must include a recognition that it's all happening within the surrounding context embracing the "mountain and peak."

The scope of our connections to our *full* environment must now be appreciated somewhat, rather than being reduced to the status of a narrow path leading into the unknown (as in FOUR). We must keep our heads up and see where we are, thoroughly experiencing our situation in Nature.

The panoramic view from the peak is important, so we must remember to head in that general direction to complete our overview or survey. As Monkey and Sage traverse and ascend the mountain, the sky or space around them becomes correspondingly more noticeable and larger than it was before. In this way, the vast context of their cultivation inevitably becomes more apparent.

This emerging context will be an increasingly central issue in the next two Stages, significantly expanding the experience of cultivation. For now, though, the panoramic quality is simply inspiring.

CONFIDENCE AND PREMATURE CONGRATULATIONS

When Monkey and Sage first come to view the mountain and satisfy themselves that they can reach it and climb it together, they believe their search is totally vindicated and nearly completed. Similarly, when we realize that the goal is not exterior to ourselves, but is founded in our fundamental nature, we feel much more calm and secure in our cultivation of life.

81

The goal seems "in hand." However, this conclusion is both correct and also somewhat misleading, since the 'mountain' still harbors many hitherto unseen 'dangers' (challenges which broaden our cultivation of the Way).

> *They may encounter 'tigers' here and, where possible, should avoid waking them. They must therefore choose carefully and intelligently from the many paths available, come to grips with unknown and powerful forces without entering into conflict, and continue their journey to the summit.*

Before Monkey and Sage can reach the peak, they must contend with various potential hazards. They must face tigers and other beasts, make their way up rock walls and across precipices, and carry on through extremes of climate. Any vast, uncharted terrain, internal or external, naturally contains such 'tigers' and 'weather.'

The skillfulness and intelligence of their relationship must now operate continuously—there's no room for even short lapses of attention or coordination. Even routes specifically mapped out by time-honored traditions to avoid these dangers still can't be followed safely without this vigilant awareness, because no map lists every detail, anticipates every contingency, or is constantly updated.

Moreover, the situation at FIVE is highly charged and multi-dimensional. By comparison, the "protective walls" of traditions' guidelines are like two-dimensional drawings, just measured out on the ground. Meanwhile, real "wild beasts" are roaming freely all around us.

KARMIC TIGERS

In general, the 'tigers' Monkey and Sage face are aspects of both themselves and the world which are not in harmony with their own mission. These beasts represent various charged factors, including 'karma'—unfinished business that threatens to embroil them in side-issues.

Such 'residues' are particularly a problem for those who have previously tried to make the path shorter by getting off at certain stages and then going directly to FIVE. Also, when we begin to address our nature more fully in FIVE, we connect to many strongly-ingrained habits and also to many potentially useful characteristics that have been ignored or left out of our approach to life in the past.

By FIVE, such neglect has given these factors a ferocious quality, a tendency to devour Monkeys and Sages, rather than just linking up with them cooperatively.

INNOCENT FEROCITY

There are still other energies, dangerous to Monkey and Sage, which are simply part of the world at large. Up to this point, Monkey and Sage have approached the path as though they were alone or unique in the world. Now they must remember that the world is not set up just to bring them, specifically, to the peak.

The world exists to fulfill the destinies of all living beings. Along the way up the mountain we may have wonderful intentions and admirable discipline, only to be devoured by a tigress who is simply hungry or needs to feed her young cubs.

We cannot, with safety, forget our own insignificance in this setting. Again, the only match for such wild, free-ranging, and sometimes indifferent ferocity is the intelligence contributed by both Monkey and Sage, finally made effective by their practiced coordination in response to the mountain's actual characteristics.

MONKEY'S VIEW

It's Monkey who tends to see the dangers of FIVE as prowling beasts, or as goblins. Even such forces as the wind or rain are mythologized by Monkey to have specific forms, temperaments, and sometimes malevolent motives ... a savagely cold, biting wind might have a white face with fangs, or a hot wind appear red, etc. To contend with these forces, Monkey must first give them some form.

As Taoists understood, with their vastly extended view of the living universe, there are many energies which do have specific characters and are further interpreted or shaped by Monkey's need to give them form. Religious mythologies, with all their bestial and anthropomorphic imagery, derive in part from Monkey's view.

Generally, Monkey's strategy is to smell dangers and climb a tree … to hide, or—if cornered, to fight. Sometimes such responses are in fact appropriate, while in other situations, such as hostile 'weather,' they may be futile gestures.

SAGE'S VIEW

Sage has studied enough traditional lore to be familiar with the mythological representation of FIVE's dangers, but prefers a more philosophical or even psychological interpretation, typically connected with notions of personal responsibility. He believes that if something appears ugly or threatening, it's due to his own character or conditioning and can be resolved or at least addressed internally.

Even when confronted with a definite external threat like a tiger, Sage may now simply "take root" on the mountain, standing so righteously in the face of danger that the tiger can't find a weakness to attack. Your destiny may be so strong at this point that even tigers can't do anything about it, so they stalk off growling because you're "too pure to eat."

PRIORITIES

Again, it's a matter of coordination between two views. The sophistication and steadiness of Sage's approach has advantages, but at times Sage must recognize that some threats are more appropriately dealt with in Monkey's terms than in his.

It's important to keep in mind that the main issue for Monkey and Sage in FIVE is not to win battles, or even to tie up all the loose ends of karma, but simply *to complete the ascent.* Often, it's best to avoid conflict, leave tigers unprovoked, and emphasize spiritual minimalism and sincerity of purpose. Otherwise, the many alternatives and issues of FIVE will prove too distracting.

In many traditions, people try to begin the Way at FIVE, and in any case don't get beyond FIVE, because they become too engrossed with interpreting all issues of Cultivation in terms of techniques, achievements, skills, strength, variations of maps of the terrain, etc. Simplicity and lack of pretense—a relaxation of striving to be something other than yourself—these are the real keys to keeping FIVE on the Way.

In the most mature and effective stage of the relationship between Monkey and Sage, Monkey ceases to be so compulsively driven by desire and Sage drops his self-righteousness. They realize that their situation is much more vast than they can ever fully understand. So their concern for each other's welfare, and their growing appreciation of both the ground and the environment of their relationship, have become more important to them than protecting and insisting on their own individual views and motives. This is an enormously important shift in priorities and perspective.

COMPASSION AND THE INCLUSIVE VIEW

Monkey and Sage have realized that even when they're blocked or threatened, adopting the most accommodating view is the best way of handling the situation and moving onward. This is a big step toward inclusive, and therefore compassionate, awareness. Such compassion is not sentimentality, but a working principle founded in a living connection between themselves and Nature. Compassion must start with ourselves and extend to the situation we're in. This makes us and our compassionate action even more effective and appropriate.

If we're not making progress or feel at odds with ourselves or our environment, it's probably just because our view of the goal is too small. We should always come back to ourselves and ask "what are we really trying to do, and why?"

Our goal should never become defined to be at odds with what we actually are. With this understanding, we can then relax all strivings based on pretense. So we become like a river—accepting what we find, filling it (living in it), rising upward, and flowing onward ... there are no obstacles to our real goal as Cultivators of the Way, only to petty achievement-oriented notions of Cultivation and of life.

As we gain some appreciation of this principle, we can apply it to others as well. So our Way is based on inclusive awareness, without pretense, and such things as compassion follow naturally from that, without needing to make an explicit goal of developing a compassionate 'attitude.'

Of course, this approach to following the Way is not the only one. People in different traditions have offered a variety of explanations of what is required—some say it's strictly compassion per se, others emphasize a pure moral force and moral conduct, still others recommend esoteric techniques or perhaps the tantric transformation of our situation and all obstacles.

One way or another, if the cultivator 'climbs' his Mountain at FIVE and thereby reaches the cloudless peak at SIX, he sees past his own dogmas and priorities, and begins to look out into the ordered proportions of Nature Itself, as it is. It's ideal if we can anticipate that discovery and make such broad accommodation the principle for cultivation all along the Way. FIVE's climb goes quickly then, and the new perspectives brought by both SIX and SEVEN are easy to assimilate.

SIX reveals the limited scope of our "goal-oriented" experience, and suggests that life itself has no such limits.

SIX

THE CLOUDLESS SUMMIT

At SIX Monkey and Sage have reached their apparent goal. Now effort ends and all innocence about the true nature of cultivation is lost in the face of a truly panoramic vision.

Monkey and Sage have reached the Cloudless Summit. That is, they've arrived at the absolute pinnacle of development permitted by a certain understanding of what they are ... and from this vantage point they have an unobstructed view of the real significance of their prior aspirations.

This is an "end of innocence," because they find that their efforts and goals are not, after all, the real issue. For, the path to SIX didn't produce anything!

Even in ONE and TWO they were already located on the distant shoulder of the mountain (the 'ground'). Now they've simply recognized the mountain that was always under foot, and have learned to tread and ascend it directly. And there isn't any treasure or exotic experience awaiting them at the peak—just a clear view of what they've always been, of where they were and where they necessarily must remain.

The horizon line of the mountain has fallen to the middle of the Image. The integrated nature uncovered by ONE through FIVE has finally emerged with sufficient clarity that its relationship with its context—the vast space of the surrounding 'sky'—is also becoming apparent.

Monkey and Sage have essentially traversed the extent of their terrain as well as they're able, exposing what they can encompass of their nature and of Nature. They've come full circle to look out over all the civilizations and forests, all the conditioned striving and primal struggles of the world, seeing these in the unfathomably vast context of the open sky.

REASSESSING THE WAY

Monkey had imagined that the size of the mountain somehow implied that gigantic bananas and other fruit were waiting at its peak. But in fact, no trees exist there, nor are any even *visible* from that great height.

However, Monkey begins to sense that the panoramic experience might itself be a source of nourishment, if he could somehow participate in it more directly. That's the challenge which engages his attention now. Compared to that possibility, the territory and fruits of his past suddenly seem small.

From FIVE, Sage had seen the peak as a podium from which he could hold forth with great speeches on the proper order of society. All his life he'd been training himself to be worthy of such a position and responsibility.

At SIX, considering the cities below, Sage is overwhelmed by the realization that trying to help people by organizing and regulating human society within such narrow parameters accomplishes little. Human dramas are played out within an immense context, which Sage now wishes to appreciate on its own terms before trying to "set the world right."

So, it's suddenly very easy for both Monkey and Sage to relinquish previous ambitions. Their relationship and the resulting panoramic vision are what they really needed, and in some respects they're perfectly satisfied now. This shows that the fruit of cultivation can never be fully anticipated or assessed from anywhere but the level of the fruit itself. It is, however, possible to anticipate the fruit of an approach by assessing the cultivator's intentions.

SIX is not at all what Monkey and Sage expected, but seen in retrospect, it is nevertheless the "logical outcome" of their desire for a great journey to fulfill their ambitions. If what they initially understood about themselves were really all that was operating as their path, SIX would in fact be the conclusion of all paths of cultivation. But because they've never yet fully appreciated themselves, and because they actually got here by emphasizing acceptance and cooperation— which are the essence of a still greater fruit—there remains the potential for further exploration of the Way, following a new and more direct approach.

GRATITUDE AND LOVE

Once at the peak, Monkey and Sage become totally calm. All action ceases. Only the wind moves, blowing over and through them.

The Image shows them quietly holding each other's hand as they take in this panoramic view. Their self-centered motives are lost, but they are fulfilled in having realized a true loving relationship. They've gone through so much together, they feel immense warmth and gratitude toward one another, and an extremely deep bond. The essence of this bond has in fact been discovered, not created.

These feelings are fully grounded, physically and energetically based. They are extended to all the beings and features of the world from which Monkey and Sage derive and which they now oversee. Their natural compassion for the world is particularly intensified by their new understanding of the dreams, humdrum busyness, and heedlessness of freedom so much in vogue below.

THE NEXT STEP

The proper next step is not to reenter the world's common preoccupations with 'fixing' and 'winning.' Rather, Monkey and Sage should continue carrying their natures (and connections with their origins) into relationship with the larger context so evident from the peak.

Monkey and Sage therefore now direct their attention to the luminous sky surrounding them, which seems encompassing in a tolerant, supportive way. They have the rather novel intuition that boundless acceptance, compassion, and love are actually being reflected *back toward* them from this Space. It's an acceptance and nurturing quality that they sense encompasses them and their world in a manner quite unknown in the earlier Stages. So they feel actively welcomed here, but in a mysteriously beckoning way that poses new challenges.

> *This environment contains no sustenance or support for them as 'Monkey' and 'Sage,' and they know they cannot stay long. To continue, they must transform themselves—that is, they must "let go" to something other than what they've always believed themselves to be.*

Monkey and Sage cannot remain at the peak … their separate characters and modes of existence can only be supported in the valleys far below them. They must therefore either return or undergo a transformation.

MASKS OVER OUR TERRAIN

In fact, only a thorough relaxation and transformation of *view* are required here. Monkey and Sage are not, as such, exactly "what we are," but masks or limited presentations of a much larger and more dynamic reality, which must now be confronted and acknowledged directly. Monkey, Sage, and the Mountain itself can now all be appreciated as having a very real connection to the "open sky" everywhere around them.

SIX is hinting that this unifying Space is what they and their activity really are—an insight that is both inspiring and daunting. It signals an end to their old views of existence and personal achievement.

Notions like 'body,' 'energy,' 'mind,' "progressing along the Way," etc., as these are seen in ONE through SIX, are only provisionally appropriate. They must now be 're-viewed,' reconsidered, in order for us to continue to receive Nature's support in following the Way as it actually is.

The important theme from the beginning has been connecting with ourselves and integrating all our various facets. And there's simply a hard limit to our ability to fit together separate pieces like 'Monkey' and 'Sage,' 'body,' 'energy,' or 'thought' per se ... because, they derive from only partial or indirect experience, and represent only fragmentary takes on our real, integrated terrain. The question now is: "How is such a shift to a totally accurate, unifying experience of ourselves possible?"

And indeed, the wind blows up from below and beckons them to fly onward. Their insights are now all-encompassing and their compassion toward others is very great. However, the very intensity of their experience begins to burn them up, apparently initiating the alchemical process that 'distills' or exposes their common, essential nature.

The 'wind' is the more primordial energy being exposed by the fusion now occurring between Monkey, Sage, Mountain, and world. Essentially, the incredible intensity of the feeling at SIX is heating and volatilizing these components, making them accessible to the full extent of the wind, the living Way of Nature.

As part of the *foundation* of their existence and of their connection with the universe, this energy-wind is now palpably felt to blow upward, from the complete range of the ground 'beneath' them, toward the larger and more open destiny represented by the sky. Thus, just when they've arrived at a position permitting them to view their world with some precision and apparent completeness, they also become exposed to new forces which move onward again, into the Unknown, toward a profound reassessment of what they are.

LETTING GO

Monkey and Sage sense that the next step in their relationship is to forfeit their individual traits, at least as perceived so far, into extinction. They feel they must bid each other goodbye, and this realization involves much sadness for them both.

In fact, the transition facing them is dramatic but not particularly drastic … it will not require their destruction, but only a shift in their status. Nevertheless, in their terms perhaps, it's a very poignant moment, with much at stake.

However, even their sadness is neutralized by the vastness of the panorama. Indeed, this neutrality is so encompassing that it is itself frightening. How can such a thoroughly impersonal view be desirable? How can a power as uncontrolled and irresistible as the wind here be good?

At SIX we feel Monkey and Sage's sadness, but also their acceptance of the Way inherent in our relationship to ourselves and Nature. We learn to accept, once and for all, that small, self-centered notions of 'desirability' and 'goodness' should be relaxed. Similarly, we come to acknowledge that things as insubstantial as the sky or wind can prevail over our own, more concrete and deliberate efforts, and may even work to a more relevant end.

We have no sane option but to trust in the living processes of Nature. We must let them operate freely, according to their own directives.

Such trust and unconditional relaxation of control instantly and effortlessly reveal SEVEN … *if* we're sensitive to the force and true intent of the 'wind' of SIX, and allow ourselves to return to our essential nature, which the wind can then take aloft. Like the ascent in FIVE, this sensitivity requires exposing more of the essential unity of our nature. However, this exposure cannot be 'done' in the ordinary sense.

The human relationship to Nature is itself overwhelming at SIX, since Nature is beginning to be seen in its real proportions. The insignificance of Monkey and Sage's little version of cooperation is very clear—it's like a bandage on a field of unbroken unity that is too huge to ever be 'done' or produced by anyone.

Those who reach SIX's peak by methods which do not emphasize harmony and unity, may still achieve vast skill and knowledge of the world below, but cannot appreciate the significance of the over-arching Space of the sky. Or, they may yearn to fly, but cannot feel the sustaining force of the 'wind.' For them, there is nothing else to do but return to the world below with their new knowledge. Many famous and influential 'spiritual' movements have in fact been started that way.

Our Monkey and Sage, on the other hand, are now well-prepared for the irrevocable release into SEVEN's encompassing Space, and do not hesitate very long in making it. And from the peak of the Mountain, which permits an unique view of every side of our existence and every aspect of the world around us, both they and their world are also seen to be within that same Space. Thus, when SEVEN opens, nothing and no one is left behind.

SEVEN is the direct experience of the limitless quality of life, the openness of complete freedom. It is entirely unmarked by goals or subjective experience.

SEVEN

SECTION I: 'ATTAINING' THE WAY

The empty frame at SEVEN shows a limitless Space, defying any definite depiction.

At SEVEN, we've made direct contact with our basic, integral nature, and have released to the primordial openness which encompasses it. Like the empty circle in the Image, the basis of our cultivation is complete, yet 'open'—without limiting or specific characteristics of any sort. SEVEN is the human relationship to Nature which involves being totally absorbed in Nature, without any parameters which could explain or define what that means ... it's like a question that resists the possibility of an answer.

LIVING WITHIN SEVEN: A SUMMARY

Whole and free from our beginningless beginning, our true nature nurtures experience at SEVEN that is open, fresh, both light and mysterious ... very plain, but also quintessentially relevant. The heavy, ponderous view of the path through SIX is gone, and so too are all other forms of toxic seriousness.

Returning to our essential nature and then opening out through it, we naturally enjoy the enormously inclusive expanse of SEVEN. This is not a matter of becoming "spaced out," dreamy or dysfunctional. Rather, the ONE-through-SIX view of life's prerequisites is revealed to be too small to really cover humanness and the human situation.

SEVEN's experience of this limitless Space isn't a particularly active phase of cultivation, and is not 'out-going' in the ordinary sense. But even if we occasionally feel a bit lost or unfocussed in SEVEN, we nevertheless also enjoy a wonderfully restorative sense of freedom from all agendas and 'purposeful' activity. Trust in Nature is fundamental, and doubts about cultivation are now banished.

Whether in formal meditation practice or in ordinary life, at SEVEN we are utterly saturated by Space. However, without our old restlessness, pressures and ambitions, this penetrating but uncharacterizable experience does not at all threaten or bore us. It is more a matter of "coming home," coming back to ourselves. SEVEN thus brings a deep sense of acceptance, joy, and compassion which previously eluded us.

Once the 'dark' (Yin) phase of SEVEN effects a profound cleansing and healing, enabling us to rest in our basic nature, the possibility of a more 'bright' (Yang) and active type of cultivation also emerges. In this way, SEVEN effortlessly opens to EIGHT through TWELVE.

THE ALCHEMY OF CULTIVATION

Monkey and Sage have been exercised (lived through) so fully that at SEVEN they and everything they represent are deeply experienced. We might say that our cultivation has encompassed and then reduced the various facets of human nature to what is really essential.

We've 'distilled' or separated out the more subtle but fundamental aspects of our nature, making them directly accessible to our attention. But we have not thereby 'achieved' anything or effected any material change.

Alchemical metaphors like 'transmutation,' 'distillation,' and 'forging' are helpful at times, especially for discussing some aspects of traditional yogic practices. However, they are linked to the issue of appreciating *completeness* or *fullness of life*. We don't need to do or get anything, but as cultivators of the Way, we may well feel like appreciating and acting from our true nature, with everything engaged.

The more complete or inclusive our experience of life, the more life's common, essential character is exposed. This in turn potentiates a still more inclusive embrace of the human relationship to Nature, and thus a deeper and more universal appreciation of essence, etc. This interplay is the basis of natural alchemy.

SEVEN is simply an effortless and comfortable settling into all the basics of life. True alchemy follows naturally from the 'cultivation' of thoroughly accommodating ourselves.

In ONE through SIX we followed the Way filtered through our preconceptions and partial experiences of our nature. In a sense, we felt limited and boxed in by our Monkey-Sage agenda and place in life, and by our apparent circumstances. We didn't attend to the rich, open Space—which includes a truly 'living' and therefore timeless Time—in which our ordinary human nature, in both its completeness and unity, always really exists.

However, the course of the Way prompted us to make better friends with ourselves, to respect and appreciate the way we actually work. So at SEVEN our basic nature is evident ... and striving is released to Space.

Such openness is both what we are, essentially, and also where we are. That is, the normal functioning of our real, integral nature expresses its freedom, its 'Space' character. Space is also 'where' that activity manifests, where it stays. There is no goal or achievement or enlightening realization in all this. It's just an acknowledgment of unconditioned openness as being both the essence and the context for a full life, Cultivating the Way.

This encompassing context, depicted in SEVEN's Image by a circle, is not a fixed or restrictive environment. Being open in all dimensions of Space and Time, it embraces everything without limiting or committing itself by doing so. The circle thus actually represents a 'sphere' of life without starting point or boundary ... an open, alchemical field.

PROGRESS?

In ONE through SIX our interaction with Nature was represented in terms of a journey proceeding over time across a diverse landscape. But in SEVEN, the old, fixed landscape has disappeared so finally and completely that we cannot refer to it meaningfully, even to say that something has happened to it. No one ever really 'enters' or even 'discovers' SEVEN. The nature and purpose of the Way are thus not what they seemed in ONE through SIX.

SEVEN has no repercussions relevant to ONE through SIX, nor is SEVEN an 'event' or 'outcome' of the journey in ONE through SIX. There is no accumulation or progress involved, no 'arrival' at SEVEN. It isn't characterized by what *apparently* came before it.

The Space emphasized at SEVEN cannot be 'achieved' or temporally positioned relative to the earlier Stages because, since it's actually their *context,* it was there all along! It manifested in a variety of forms, like the 'sky' which Monkey and Sage saw to be accommodating and nurturing them and their world, while enticing them to avoid stagnation, to cleave to livingness.

Stages ONE through SIX were described as situations and journeys made by individual characters. But SEVEN through TWELVE celebrate various facets of the field or Space which is a central aspect of the fully-integrated human relationship to Nature. All of the later Stages are thus real, enduring features of our situation, from the 'beginning' at ONE.

The movements, 'progress,' and 'arrivals' of a 'discoverer' within this Space and these Stages do have some interest, and can be discussed for some purposes. However, they are not the whole story or the main point.

A NOTE ON THE 'EXPERIENCE' OF CULTIVATION

ONE through SIX sees cultivation as a movement, by a cultivator, who has progressively more profound experiences along the Way. But we do not tell the story of SEVEN through TWELVE as involving an heroic journey onward and upward, with "bigger and better" experiences at every stage. For, the cultivator does not move away from us ordinary mortals.

We cannot say that SEVEN through TWELVE are later than ONE through SIX, or that the cultivator's central 'experiences' of the Stages are specific cognitive events which involve him and not other human beings. But in deference to ordinary language, we'll continue to refer to the 'experience' of each Stage. The term 'experience' has the advantage of suggesting an integrated participation in life, unlike words like 'knowledge,' 'understanding,' or even 'perception' which tend to suggest something apprehended only with one's mind or senses.

However, we must emphasize that 'experience' is being used in a new way. It no longer indicates something exclusively done or possessed by a particular person at a particular time, nor does it exclude 'seeing,' 'appreciating,' a certain degree of 'understanding,' etc. The cultivator's full, forged nature is always engaged and connected to the human situation at large.

The cultivator's 'experience' in SEVEN through TWELVE is not a special sensation or state or affect induced by some process. It's the subtlety of the "human experience" itself, the experience in which all human life participates, at every Stage.

SEVEN

SECTION II: THE HUMAN EXPERIENCE

In emphasizing the context of all twelve Stages, SEVEN brings forward a central dimension of the "human experience" in general, not a new, special, or extraordinary experience. Thus, 'experiencing' SEVEN does not reactivate or stimulate our old feelings of self importance.

VESTIGES OF SELF IMPORTANCE

Prior to SEVEN, Monkey and Sage dominated our cultivation of the Way, while acting from a fundamental unity and capacity that became increasingly evident as their relationship unfolded. But they continued to believe that they, as individual characters, must still figure prominently in the rest of Cultivation.

In the last and most subtle forms of such self importance, they felt that *they* must have a special experience which transcends their normal view, that *they* must be transcended, or must 'die' to make way for further 'unifying' progress. This residual self importance finally 'peaks' at SIX, and at SEVEN is balanced by natural self respect for the full extent of what we really are.

The significance of SIX as a transition to SEVEN is that all emphasis on peak experiences or transcendent realizations must be relaxed. No transcendence scheme is among the major issues unfolding beneath the overarching sky of FIVE and SIX. Nor do Monkey and

Sage have to 'die' or change to clear the way for something truly central and fundamental like Cultivation of the Way.

Our successful Cultivation is already going on twenty-four hours a day. It's the functioning of our full, integrated nature or terrain in its relationship to Nature.

ONE through SIX just made this cooperative relationship more apparent, so Monkey and Sage could relax. That may be assisted by contemplative or yogic practice, but daily life can also make the same point quite effectively.

Monkey and Sage were able to relax at the end of SIX because it became clear that their self preservation was neither in jeopardy nor an issue for obsessive concern. The journey to SIX showed that cultivation is not a matter of overcoming or holding on to anything, but of *including* more of what we are. This inclusive approach holds no overriding or paralyzing threat so long as the small Monkey-Sage views and territories are respected as we open to embrace larger ones.

By acknowledging their fundamental connection to Nature at SIX, Monkey and Sage—though perhaps sad and apprehensive—found that they can trust Nature to hold them up, while It also encompasses other regions of the human terrain. This trust is fundamental to the remainder of the Way, reaching its most dramatic—but still quite *human*—expressions in the lives of the Earthly and Heavenly Immortals at TEN and ELEVEN.

OPENING TO HUMANNESS

At SEVEN we begin to be comfortable with our humanness as it is, finding it to be completely founded in Nature Itself, superlative in every way. By contrast, although very human in their idiosyncrasies, Monkey and Sage don't represent humanness fully.

Monkey is, after all, a "wild beast" of sorts, and Sage has pretensions to godliness ("perfectibility beyond humanness"). In SEVEN, opening past such small aspirations, we use the larger perspective of SEVEN's

Space to operate as human beings. It's precisely by leaving nothing out that we see that nothing really needs to be excluded or changed.

Partial, disintegrated experience of humanness casts us as Monkey and therefore we feel 'treed,' restless. Similarly, as Sage we are controlled but rather conservative or 'landbound,' obsessed with steady improvement along proper lines. But in SEVEN, we're united with the rising ground of humanness and the human agenda, which, like a Mountain, naturally and obviously exists in relation with the surrounding 'sky' or Space.

That relationship is now confirmed or sealed. So we see that we've been exercising our humanness and freedom all along, but have far more scope for doing so than we previously noticed.

Monkey, Sage, and the Mountain are now one with this Space.

What was really essential about Monkey and Sage is inseparable from the open Space or atmosphere here, which enjoys true freedom, without death. In that sense, they too partake in the vast movements within the living dimensions of open Space and timeless Time. In fact, they have always resided in these dimensions, and nothing in any Stage has ever blocked that realization.

NO OBSTACLES

At the end of SIX, Monkey and Sage were literally *surrounded* by an understanding of the need for humble capitulation to a more accurate and open view. But this resignation means dropping *both* our conceits about being distinct minds, potent egos, spiritual souls, etc., *and* our ideas of being good or bad, strong or weak. When we drop our self-importance, we drop our ambitions *and* our concerns about being flawed, needing to be improved and 'forged.'

Paradoxically, if we cling to self importance, we can always find alleged obstacles and reasons for feeling excluded from the Space of SEVEN— our posture is not perfect, or we don't have "enough chi," or still have thoughts and emotions, sleep lying down, lack certain specialized meditation experiences, are not martial arts champions, wear eyeglasses, etc. The list of possible shortcomings is endless and fairly silly.

However, as we've seen, SEVEN is simply the open-ended experience of our forged or *integral* nature, our very ordinary nature "taken all at once" without pretence or striving. The basic components of our existence are forged from the beginning—*not* perfect, because life is not really about being perfect, but partaking in a definite unity and quite "O.K." This experience is both the basis and the fruit of cultivating the Way.

If instead we approach cultivation based on the small view that we must work to create the fruit of life, then we see it as a matter of narrowing—squinting and straining—to make something happen inside 'our' body and energy. This approach distorts both life and yogic practices, making them hazardous struggles—more Monkey fights and exercises in Sagely self-discipline—rather than natural examples of self-expression.

SEVEN opens up the field of our exploration. The fruit is not really to be found 'inside' us or our ordinary senses of logic, space, or time—rather, we and our situations *are in it!* We don't have to 'move' toward it or clear away obstacles to realizing it.

We should practice cultivation accordingly ... not squinting and squirming, but simply respecting our entire nature while keeping our "heads up and eyes open." We then automatically experience the atmosphere or Space where life really unfolds. We feel how natural it is that people ignore this context, but also how natural and effortless it is to acknowledge it. After all, the open field of all life is not something that could really be more available to one human existence than another.

PERSONAL AND UNIVERSAL FREEDOM

For some cultivators, SEVEN is initially experienced as the openness of our basic nature and its context or "personal environment." Traditionally, our open nature-in-context is called the 'shen.' Thus, in referring to 'Space' so far, we've actually been talking about an aspect of the shen.

Like the sky shown in SIX, the shen encompasses our entire existence. It summarizes what the functioning of our nature, including our body and energy, "adds up to." And what each life really adds up to is an individual expression of the Tao. The shen is the integral nature of an individual life, both the essence and the totality of each person's being, first seen in its open (Space) manifestation.

The shen is, in one sense, the Space of the full terrain of our lives. Without 'acting,' it nevertheless contextualizes our actions, grounding our motive for fully 'returning' to the Source. This 'return' is simply a demonstration of our true position as human beings.

This shen/Space is thus like a *personal* or *local* region of the infinite open Space of SEVEN, a "little tao" which naturally wants to capitalize itself by becoming "the Tao"—by acknowledging that in our integral nature there's nothing separating us from the rest of Space. SEVEN makes it clear that this 'capitalization' is not aggrandizement, only clarity about our situation.

While for some cultivators, SEVEN is primarily a personal, 'shen' experience, others move directly to the appreciation of SEVEN as the open Space in which *all* of Nature manifests. This is possible because the shen has no real boundary separating it from the Tao. Thus, SEVEN is more than just our personal, local neighborhood of freedom. It's a far larger and more universal 'context.' Of course, both the personal and universal views of SEVEN are important, and either may be cultivated first.

> This is the motionless open Space which includes all phenomena
> before, during, and after their myriad manifestations.

Everything is here but is, as yet, undifferentiated and unseen. This nameless Space does not deny or undermine things, but is for that very reason far too *inclusive* to exhibit any particular characteristics. Even if we see SEVEN as something much vaster than the shen/Space of our personal environment, it still seems empty here.

Universes are as specks of dust in this Space, not easily detected in the vastness. Also, no one exclusive "point of view" is left to "find something" in this Space ... in SEVEN, we're there along with every-thing else, and so nothing predominates or asserts its view.

In the next section, we'll consider this 'emptiness' and its relation to the rest of the Way.

SEVEN

SECTION III: ALTERNATIVE STRATEGIES AT SEVEN

SEVEN is best appreciated if the complete path of ONE through SIX has been followed, without 'skipping.' For, such thoroughness shows that SEVEN is not the result of self-improvement and isn't a radical departure from what we really were in ONE through SIX. Its impact is therefore fulfilling and significant.

ALTERNATIVE APPROACHES TO SEVEN

Although it runs contrary to Taoists' practice and sense of timing, SEVEN may also be glimpsed directly 'from' any of the previous stages up through FIVE. In that case, the experience *does* tend to seem like a breakthrough, a departure from our normal reality, particularly from the concreteness of ordinary situations. SEVEN is then quite shocking, difficult to assimilate.

Leaping 'into' SEVEN at unpredictable intervals and losing sight of it again may seem appealingly 'mystical,' but doesn't really contribute much to our cultivation. Proper cultivation is a matter of effortless continuity, of living in the fruit with all that we are. The requisite continuity is not continuous effort or vigilance, but the continuity of our living terrain and its seamless relationship with Nature.

SEVEN is almost never entered from TWO or ONE, but when this does happen, Sage feels assaulted by an unruly and evil chaos, and

Monkey falls out of his tree (rather than climbing down willingly) and thus blacks out. The Source is then mistaken, as in a nightmare, for a dark and terrifying enemy.

Even those who enjoy the full grounding of ONE through SIX may sometimes find SEVEN a little intimidating.

CONFRONTING THE WAY'S MIDNIGHT PHASE

Opening toward the heart of SEVEN, we first encounter the ultimate development of the Yin aspect of the Tao in phenomena. It may appear 'dark,' like midnight with no moon in the sky.

From one point of view, Yin may be associated with conceptual thinking and the proliferation of distinctions and insights. But by SEVEN, that aspect has grown so intense it has essentially snuffed itself out, leaving 'nothing' that can be seen or thought in the old way. SEVEN can thus seem negative or even frightening, apparently undermining what an unsophisticated meditator may seek to cultivate or maintain.

SEVEN is traditionally associated with the onset of what is sometimes called the Third Eye. The first two Eyes are related to the erratic quality of Monkey at ONE and the conservative steadiness of the Sage at TWO. The Third Eye, then, is a more balanced eye on fundamentals, on our relationship to the Tao, which we've already discussed in general terms. However, the Yin facet of the scene at SEVEN, as revealed to this Third Eye, is a non-dual and unoriginated reality, empty of independent 'things' and undisturbed by particular events.

It is possible to visit SEVEN and be so disoriented by the Yin 'void' aspect of this experience that one instinctively returns, dazed, to SIX or even FIVE. However, for a cultivator with a sound experience of his integral nature, this retrenchment back to a more 'solid' position is generally unnecessary.

HUNTING AND FLEEING THE MYSTERIOUS

People have held a variety of attitudes about SEVEN, sometimes even fixating on the mysterious, empty, dark aspects of its Yin character. Those who believe that the point of cultivation is to plunge into mysteries actually pursue this Yin. Others fear Yin 'emptiness' as being an enemy of life and light.

In fact, 'mystery' is not a sensible goal, and the Yin at this Stage is only a problem if one becomes obsessed with it rather than leaving it in its natural context of transformation. At its most intense phase, in the very heart of SEVEN, the Yin naturally turns around again, yielding to the Yang aspect of the Way. (The latter, in turn, will expose another, even more profoundly 'spiritual Yin' in the later Stages, on the Way to a truly nondual experience.)

RESISTING A COMPLETE EXPERIENCE

Those who do have difficulties *after* entering SEVEN have usually not approached it in a way that makes the experience full and applicable to life. People also occasionally arrive in SEVEN and then deliberately "throw on the breaks," closing themselves to the natural process of continuing growth. Essentially, they decline to acknowledge or participate in any further 'tendencies,' particularly those which lead toward the reintroduction of some sort of phenomena.

By clinging to SEVEN's center, these people reject the Yang force which inevitably enters SEVEN in its proximity to EIGHT and entices us into EIGHT through TEN. So they actually fight the continuation of the Way itself.

THE THRESHOLD TO REBIRTH

From the vantage points of ONE through SIX, SEVEN does *seem* like it would be a place of equanimity, free of any disturbances, or possibly a Yin 'Void.' Actually, SEVEN is a very powerful place—the threshold to a new beginning.

If SEVEN seems *dark,* that's simply because it's a "clean slate." It's *empty* only in the sense that it is an openness which is full of power, free of limits. This is the proper function of the Yin in Cultivating the Way. The Space of SEVEN is thus not a vacuum, but the mysterious womb of energy.

When fully appreciated, SEVEN is the stage of Return which removes many limits and obstacles to seeing the Source as the creative energy that produces everything. In SEVEN's Space, emptiness and form are continuously at play in a storm of potentialities. Those who deliberately focus on only one aspect of this Space, and resist participating in the tendencies toward further exposure of its potency, essentially deny the very foundation of creation.

Some people take this position because they feel phenomena and their source to be tainted, perhaps a distraction from something 'higher' or transcendent. Or they fear that the power of creation is too seductive and must be renounced lest it corrupt them.

Meditators may also believe that if they're going to reenter movement or look in a particular direction again, it should be in the direction of SIX. From SIX's mountain peak, they feel they could at least exercise compassion for all the fellow human beings seen milling about below.

Those who resist "SEVEN neighboring EIGHT" demonstrate a prejudiced stance toward the complete human experience and toward Nature Itself. They use a small, 'heroic' notion of compassion as an excuse to resist Nature's full instructions. If maintained with sufficient stubbornness, such incomplete views result in exhaustion, perversely ('heroically') swimming against the stream leading to union with the Source.

THE 'METEOR' STRATEGY

There is yet another important reason why some people fight moving on toward EIGHT. This resistance can itself fuel a leap to the completion of the Way ... or so people both within and outside of Taoism have claimed.

The power of SEVEN near EIGHT expresses itself in many different directions simultaneously. It's wild, ferocious, bringing forth everything and also devouring itself.

Thus, you can even direct SEVEN's power to avoid becoming powerful! By maintaining your position in the face of an ever-accumulating power until you either fail to "hold out" or a normal death finally occurs, you may succeed in going directly into TWELVE ... at any rate, that's the idea.

This strategy was called "Ch'an Taoism" by my (Charles's) teachers in Taiwan. It's motivated by a desire to avoid any possible entrapment in the complexities beginning at EIGHT. It thus renounces resolving karmic loose ends by working with the naked energies in EIGHT through ELEVEN. Instead it holds that a surer method is to build up such a potent Yang charge in SEVEN that one eventually shoots out, like a meteor, into TWELVE. This approach is thus the most explicit and deliberate version of the notion of meditation as *waiting* (but 'waiting' in timeless Time).

Perhaps something of this idea does underlie some meditative lineages within various traditions. In any case, it's a rather controversial point. Several of my teachers in Taiwan maintained that there *are* things to encounter, resolve, and complete, just because all of Nature's dynamics must be fully acknowledged in Cultivating the Way. This is the agenda of EIGHT through ELEVEN.

Another of my teachers actually claimed that, in any case, you never do acquire a charge which shoots you through to TWELVE, but only one which conveys you to the threshold of the next stage. In his view, the force accumulated by the 'meteor' strategy simply serves to propel you *very quickly* from Stage to Stage, so the details of the traversed terrain are sometimes missed.

CULTIVATING PRIMORDIAL COMPASSION

It may be safest to say that although "Ch'an Taoism" is a legitimate method for some people, it isn't appropriate for everyone. Moreover, there's another issue which becomes increasingly important in the Stages following SEVEN—the intention of the cultivator, and this individualizes one's strategy in cultivation.

The highest—the most natural—intention behind going on, into power is to demonstrate fearless acceptance of the complete human relationship to Nature, and to inspire all living beings. The ultimate expression of such compassion is to unreservedly enter the Source of all life, potency, and inspiration, which then inevitably reaches out to enfold and support others in their own Cultivation of the Way.

Compassion is thus most appropriately linked to the shen's nurturing the body and energy while preserving their connection to the Tao itself. The shen's compassion supports our lives and access to the unlimited life of the Tao.

As cultivators of the Way, we are not separate from Nature's own nurturing power, but can actually *contribute* to it and express it with our entire being. This intention cannot be manufactured, but when it arises naturally, it should be respected and followed. In this way, we open to EIGHT and the other remaining Stages.

EIGHT is the orderly simplicity of life felt in a broad, energetic way, framed only in terms of universal principles.

EIGHT

SECTION I: THE LAWS OF NATURE

The Image of EIGHT is a symbolic depiction of the true and fundamental patterns of energy which constitute the Laws of Nature.

Eventually, the featureless inactivity of SEVEN gives way to subtle stirrings in the early Yang phase of the Way. This is the onset of EIGHT.

A 'cool' vision prevailed in SEVEN's central region, totally open but uncommitted to anything. When SEVEN's absence of feeling finally negated *even* itself, an intense energy that could no longer remain cool—the Yang aspect of SEVEN's Space—then reached out into the area bordering EIGHT, and finally into the experience of EIGHT.

THE EMERGING STRUCTURE OF NATURE

As our integrated awareness burns through to EIGHT, it appreciates with great precision that the Space of SEVEN is not empty. Our experience also suggests that SEVEN's energy is not, after all, expressed only randomly or in chaos.

EIGHT shows the basic structure or 'skeleton' of the universe. Even if it seemed at times that SEVEN's Space was a 'Void,' EIGHT is its "operational structure," exposed by our growing sensitivity to the pattern of 'light' in this Space. The duet of Yin and Yang, the multi-faceted play of the Five Elements or fundamental types of energy ... these and other aspects of the Laws of Nature, depicted in the Image, are all revealed in their naked presence.

The myriad creations deriving from these Laws are still hidden in the mists. Only the essential patterns show through quite prominently, so the human relationship to Nature here is the deep participation in life's fundamental patterns. EIGHT is the basic geometry, the 'theorems,' of Nature.

Our discovery of this geometry clarifies the process of cultivation running through the earlier Stages. The subtle principles underlying ritual, yogic, and contemplative methods are now obvious. We essentially recognize the source of the efficacy of all contemplative and yogic practices.

Most importantly, like all the other Stages, EIGHT helps put the events and processes of ordinary life into perspective. We can now know, at least in general, how things work and why. In that 'knowing,' there is no resistance to the way things are.

> *(the Laws) are difficult to understand completely and yet operate freely within us, ordering and reordering our relationship to Nature.*

EIGHT is the acceptance of what Taoists call Great Order. Before EIGHT, this acceptance would be, at best, a mere belief or attitude of the sort that often characterizes popularizations of Taoism ("trust Nature," "be natural," etc.). But by apprehending this Order directly, both within and outside of ourselves, we participate in it thoroughly and therefore—to an increasing degree in the next few Stages of the path—become able to play in harmony with every aspect of life.

Strictly speaking, since neither 'we' as subjects nor individual things as 'objects' are in view at EIGHT, EIGHT's experience cannot be explicitly associated with something occurring inside or outside 'us.' However, it is a deeply experiential understanding of all natural process, and in that sense, it embraces every aspect of any particular living being or thing, just as it does the entire Universe.

The 'cultivator' shown at EIGHT *is* the Laws of Nature demonstrating Great Order, not a person *using* it. EIGHT is not an active stage in the personal sense, so we certainly don't seek to use the forces revealed at EIGHT to make ourselves comfortable or to promote ourselves in some selfish way.

The insight that there is no self, no experiencer, is now fully developed. At SEVEN this insight was quite concrete but basically cast in more negative terms—the Monkey and Sage were unmasked, released into their open context, whereas at EIGHT the actual dynamics of that context are clearly seen and appreciated.

This is a truly positive discovery, because nothing is rejected or disregarded. Moreover, in this openness of self and 'things' there is the basis for unencumbered expression and development.

Life—which is both the object and the very operation of Taoist cultivation—is seen to proceed directly through the operation of EIGHT's principles. This is not a description of some "higher existence," as opposed to ordinary life. Ordinary life can do without the crude, inefficient notions of subject, object, and actions. And if they arise, that's also fine—efficiency is not the main issue, and Great Order is preserved in either case. No one, no thing, gets in the way, or prevents the play of ordinary life from being the effortless process of the Way's *completion* (traditionally called *wu wei*).

FINISHING UP

People generally want to use their energy to *do* or *produce* something. This tendency is natural and sometimes important but, in the form it usually takes, is also somewhat self-limiting. SEVEN profoundly relaxed and suspended this urge. EIGHT then goes on to *finish* our involvement in 'ambitious' pursuits, which ignore the fact that the Way is already fully operating.

Great Order is not a static state of 'tidiness,' but allows for a joyous expression of freedom. Prior to SEVEN and EIGHT, we often feel that the conditions of our lives have created messes, problems, or limitations. Therefore, we may first appreciate Great Order at EIGHT as

being a natural dynamic for settling our ambitions and their consequences, and also the subtler indulgence of feeling limited by them.
Even the ambition of "transcending ambition" is concluded. But
'finishing' isn't really 'stopping' ... it just means that the living Space
of SEVEN and EIGHT compassionately embraces the various tendencies of our nature while emphasizing *essential* human experience,
the ground and main thrust of all life.

This view of Great Order depends on seeing things in their full context. In the later Stages, we can then *apply* this rather impersonal
vision, characteristic of EIGHT, in many different ways. We can
express ourselves with vigor and freedom in all the worlds of conditions, of Yin and Yang and the Five Elements.

Approached from the views of the early Stages, these Elemental
factors do indeed seem like conditioning influences, sources of
dualism, conflict, trouble. But even our initial experience of EIGHT
shows that they are really quite "in order." When recognized in this
way, our usual accumulations of ambition based on dissatisfaction
and regimens of improvement come to an end forever.

THE ORDER IN ORDINARY LIFE

Even ordinary life shows Great Order very clearly, if we care to experience it. But of course, in the earlier Stages we often prefer to ignore
it or assume that it's missing. By adopting a narrow view, we take
exception to what arises, decide that intervention is required to set
things right, and initiate long sequences of corrective action. Such
intervention and 'correction' may not really fix anything that needs
fixing, and probably miss the point being made by Great Order.

Let's consider a simple example taken from our approach to handling emotions. We typically repress such emotions as anger, finding them to be embarrassing, 'wrong,' or even dangerous. In the same
way, we may seek out or emphasize other emotions. If fact, such preferences come from reacting to labels we paste on energies which, in
themselves, are fine (but not 'good' or 'bad').

If we look directly, without bias, we may see a particular type of anger as an manifestation of, say, the Fire element in our energy. And as such, taken in context, it's magnificent. It can exhibit an admirable precision, aptly completing an interaction or communication, leaving no conflict which carries over into subsequent moments. Our position is thus properly expressed, and nothing is left undone or unsaid.

Such anger is creative, not 'destructive' in a problematical sense. Why then does anger usually seem dangerous to us? Because we normally overlay it so heavily with negative and highly-charged 'fronts' (labels) that we suppress it, building up a large accumulation of residues from previous situations.

Such an accumulation is indeed dangerous, in a sense, because it motivates explosive reactions which aren't appropriate to the particular situation at hand—'over-reactions' to labels, not reality. It can also lead to endless echoes, cycles of "action and reaction," again involving residues deriving from our unwillingness to see the real, naked energies at play.

EIGHT's precision helps us realize, once and for all, the folly of trying to fight or fix our natures. If we resist the impulse to fight natural processes, we see that apparent 'problems' aren't problems at all, and will in any case be resolved or meet their balancing counterparts as a matter of course. The real issue is thus to understand the full scope of what is happening. We may then enter into it, and even 'assist' where necessary.

The point of nonintervention or nonaction in EIGHT is not to stand aloof from everything. It's to participate actively in ways that express our own role in the operation of Great Order.

FULFILLMENT IN ORDINARY LIFE

This new approach to life differs markedly from that common at ONE, in which we accumulated various factors in pursuit of some small goal, never really feeling what we were doing very deeply. We achieved something only to become dissatisfied with it ... and so we started again.

At EIGHT, *all* our hungers and pursuits are seen to be working toward fulfillment. They constitute a process of completion, not a pattern of continuous effort. We can find satisfaction, but without producing a compulsion to "do it again." Nothing is conditioned to reappear.

The play of the Yin and Yang and the Elements is thus not just the basis for the manifestation of dualistic phenomena *from* the Source, but is also the Way of Return *to* the Source. This play is both the path and the "following of the Path." Great Order and the Elements are the completers as well as the initiators, and the burden of progressing or of fixing things has never been an issue at all.

EIGHT

SECTION II: THE CULTIVATOR'S INTEGRITY OF ACTION

In SEVEN through TWELVE, the Way clearly reveals itself as the path of completion for *all* phenomena, not just for ourselves. Again, the 'cultivator' is no longer an 'individual' in the isolated, Monkey-versus-Sage sense, but is understood to include everything operating in the human relationship to Nature.

The Image at EIGHT is still simply a circle, like SEVEN. But now we see the pillars of Yin and Yang as defining the Gate of Duality, supported by the Element-steps, all actively leading to a complete Return.

Through this Gate of Duality we have an unobstructed view of the unbroken integrity of the Source. In that integrity, the need for fiddling and adjusting things is extinguished. If at EIGHT we begin our preparations for using the Five Elements to play, it's not because we need to change anything, and involves no presumptuous meddling with some forbidden or tainted power.

Many people have preferred to stay in SEVEN, rejecting the power which is founded in EIGHT and actively used by Taoists in the later stages. For, such activity is often misunderstood as dabbling in sorcery.

It's true that EIGHT shows *everything* participating in Great Order, so both our own actions and Nature's processes in general can spontaneously bring things to completion. And this does encourage us to expand the scope of our activity in NINE and TEN in extraordinary ways. We thus become connected to the livingness of our environment in a much larger sense. But such actions simply seal and express the respect for ourselves and Nature which first began to grow in FOUR. The potency and integrity of all natural processes are quite distinct from the petty manipulativeness which often dominates attempts at sorcery.

STRUCTURE AND OPENNESS, LAWS AND FREEDOM

Another reason people have avoided acknowledging the principles revealed in EIGHT is that their operation might seem incompatible with both the open-dimensional nature of reality, and with our own freedom. The whole idea of "Laws of Nature" normally seems to imply some kind of inflexible, mechanical process involving a particular, determinate Nature or Universe.

Here the logic and perception common to ONE through SIX fail us in our attempt to understand 'natural process.' Normally, we think that a situation exhibits either determinism or randomness. There appear to be no other options. And how can 'laws' be the basis for freedom?

Taoists see the 'laws' at EIGHT not as obscuring factors or compellers, but as pointing directly to the open nature and full character of SEVEN's Space and of Nature generally ... they don't constrain, they *express* and *facilitate*. They are the core dynamics of the way of freedom. We only become unfree to the extent that we fail to appreciate and participate in their operation (i.e., in our own living dimension).

Those who deny this may be simply clinging to SEVEN, refusing to look closely and without bias at its actual character. These laws not only manifest our particular situation but provide access to limitless other possibilities. They are the source of our freedom because they connect us to Nature Itself. In Nature, true freedom inheres as a central facet of 'being,' not just as the basis for a little self's decisions and ability to perform some action.

People sometimes try to define freedom in absurd terms, that go against the grain of the Great Order of our nature and situation, just so they can feel unfree and thus shed the burden of real freedom within Order.

Many of the things people associate with 'freedom' are tantamount to saying that we should be able to eat with our ears or walk on our faces. Such unnatural definitions of freedom don't really preserve or protect the freedom of our human nature or our opportunity to cultivate the Way, living a full and meaningful life. We should trust that precisely such natural actions as walking on our feet rather than our faces are what effectively express our connection to real freedom, as represented by EIGHT.

EXTENDING THE THIRD EYE'S VIEW

EIGHT's view of Great Order and of the living structure of SEVEN's open space continues the maturation of the Third Eye. While the Yin facet of this vision, stressing 'emptiness' or 'space,' characterized SEVEN, EIGHT begins an emphasis on the positive Yang facet associated with the potency of this space. The completely open Third Eye sees the simultaneity and inseparability of emptiness and patterns, of openness and definite principles, of our individual microcosms and the Tao.

In Taoism, the Third Eye's vision is not a final goal. It is, however, greatly respected, since it provides us with a firm foundation for a safe and balanced approach to further investigations into the fullness of our relationship to Nature. Without this foundation, we could fall prey to fantasies and obsessions when confronted with the enormous range of possibilities available beginning at EIGHT.

THE FOURTH EYE'S VIEW OF THE LIVING UNIVERSE

Our new investigations at EIGHT are tentative uses of yet another Eye founded in our relationship to Nature. With the acceptance of EIGHT's principles, this increasingly active Fourth Eye sees that Nature's openness is not only structured and well-ordered, but also alive and *populated.*

Nature often seems to people like a mere container or a life-support machine for various living organisms. But in fact, every aspect of Nature is alive. Even Space, Time, and Matter are all alive, and open in scope.

123

'Inert' and 'empty' regions or things are only projections of a particular view, impoverished by a limited participation in Nature's living dimension. Rocks and tables and the flame of a candle are all nonsentient objects of the rather rigid forms of attention available to Monkey and Sage in the earlier stages. But at EIGHT, all 'objects' are understood to be masks on a living continuum, and in that sense, to be flexible and alive themselves.

Nature's livingness also includes an entitative aspect, abundantly manifest in the lives of many types of sentient beings. Such beings are born of different energy matrices and patterns, inhabiting different spaces within the Space we first encounter at SEVEN. Moreover, even things which would not typically be considered as 'beings,' but rather as forces or processes of Nature, impinge upon us on many levels and can be related to as entities (if we wish to take that approach). Taoism and other ancient traditions offer many methods for doing this, all founded in EIGHT and NINE.

Neither individual human beings nor the individual beings of other realms are the explicit objects of the Fourth Eye's attention at EIGHT. At this point only the 'spoor,' the basic indications of the presence and patterns of various *types* of beings, are revealed. The general features of their characteristic natures and traces become apparent here, but their precise forms (as they would appear to us) have not yet emerged.

EIGHT's consideration of enormous numbers of universes of different types of entities doesn't belittle the status of human beings or the human view—it establishes them both more clearly by putting humanness in perspective. Exposing our natural connections to the living universe enriches our acceptance of humanness, rather than inciting us to chase or conjure contacts with 'superhuman' creatures out of a sense of inferiority.

Beginning at EIGHT, therefore, we can assess and enjoy humanness in a truly balanced way, by comparing our own nature and environment with those of other types of sentient beings. We can also relate more directly to the general livingness of Nature in this way. This possibility of a new, *interpersonal* kind of friendship with Nature is founded at EIGHT and becomes an increasingly important, concrete aspect of the Way in NINE and TEN.

SEEING LIFE'S VARIETY WITHOUT BIAS

The assessment available here is based on a much larger vision than that enjoyed by Sage and Monkey at SIX, overlooking their world from the mountain peak. Their view was truly panoramic, but extended within only a small set of the dimensions for perception and living actually inherent in the human relationship to Nature.

When SIX is taken as a goal in itself, disconnected from continuing natural processes, it provides a poor basis for considering actions and alternatives in cultivating the Way. By contrast, the Fourth Eye at EIGHT penetrates the surface of things and shows us, with great precision, how life and the Way of Nature operate, and where we as human beings fit in the living universe.

At SIX the sadness of looking directly at peoples' lives and limiting circumstances motivated a kind of sympathetic compassion. SEVEN unmasked the ground of compassion, but opened quite beyond the issue of compassion as involving pity, concern, or identifiable action. EIGHT returns to the issue, exposing both the true nature of all actions and the uncontrived compassion inherent within them. At EIGHT, our insight into the processes at work and the enormity of the *full* human situation brings ordinary 'sympathy' to an end. For, in the perception of Great Order, we drop all judgment and ordinary partiality.

We see the unfolding of this Order everywhere, and realize that no one is really stuck. Just as there are no lifeless regions in Nature, there are no dead ends. But this appreciation of Great Order and the absence of judgment don't necessarily make us aloof or *unmoved* by events. Our hearts go out to all *livingness,* as it is and as it's actually connected to us, and so our reactions cease to be conditioned, predictable, or provincial.

People typically restrict their sympathy to parents, close relations, or friends, but the cultivator maturing at EIGHT might experience tremendous feeling for a mountain. He may find the 'dying' of an ember in a fire worthy of a deep emotional response, while the tragic events that figure in newspapers' headlines may elicit no reaction at all ... in the latter 'tragedies' he may simply see things being brought to their proper completion and feel no connection with them that requires a personal response. He views everything as "straw dogs," like the straw figures used in rituals of ancient times in place of animal sacrifice. So, everything is experienced, not at all as *valueless,* but as participating in "precious insignificance."

The happiness and sadness, the Yang and Yin phases, of someone at EIGHT are themselves intimately connected both to phenomena and to Great Order. They are thus quite inscrutable to people who focus only on the surface and are unaware of the factors prompting their own conditioned reactions.

THE INSPIRATION AND TECHNOLOGY GROUNDING ALL TEACHINGS

The behavior of the cultivator at EIGHT, while strange at times, is also highly instructive. For, here we participate in the origin of all accurate instruction, and see directly how various methods of cultivating the Way operate. In some cases, we may discover that they do not, in fact, still operate, or that they're inappropriate for one person and ideal for another.

During my (Charles's) training in Taiwan, and rather to my dismay, one of my teachers frequently tossed aside particular teachings I had received from others. To state his claim in the terms of this book, he said that since he could take up the vantage points of EIGHT and NINE, he could evaluate such teachings without just indulging in personal prejudices.

I frequently tried to "speak for the defense," explaining other peoples' points of view and reasons for taking a certain approach ... but often, my teacher would just say "No! They're wrong!" without any hesitation or apology. When I showed him prints of various figures important to another meditation tradition, he would correct the details of the forms based on his own encounters with these entities

... occasionally, he would even say something like "oh, *he* isn't there anymore!" (that is, such-and-such an entity is no longer 'operative' or appearing as a certain fundamental aspect of Nature).

This teacher said that when I experienced what we're here calling Great Order, I would understand and would assess things with equal confidence, automatically accepting the responsibilities associated with such knowledge. There was no room for discussion or differences of opinion ... just for insight and, eventually, in NINE and TEN, *action*.

THE RESPONSIBILITY OF "TRUE CULTIVATORS OF THE WAY"

Many Taoists—particularly those involved in the practice of trance mediumship—have agreed with the teacher mentioned above that the Fourth Eye provides a view that is not optional. To such masters, someone who refuses involvement in its complex reality is both shirking a major responsibility and also being unrealistic. My teacher essentially said "If you won't accept this, go sit in SEVEN ... see how long you can stay there!"

SEVEN can only be clung to as a refuge from our own natural maturation if we ignore its true character, and in that case we risk sliding backward even further to SIX and earlier stages. Traditions basing their views and virtues on SIX are building on a small and unstable ground, inadequate to support a complete understanding of compassion or of cultivating the Way.

Once someone at EIGHT has witnessed Great Order and operated consciously within its patterns, there is no way to 'fall' backward. For, at this point we recognize that *going forward or backward are both patterns within Great Order.* So even if we find ourselves moving back to manifest life in the previous Stages, it's only another aspect of a necessary completion process, and we don't see those Stages in a prejudicial light.

We can never lose our Way, because all the possible relationships to Nature, represented by the twelve Stages, contribute to it. Only with this realization and the confidence it brings can we accept our responsibilities as "true cultivators of the Way."

EIGHT

SECTION III: THE YOGIC IMPULSE AT EIGHT

Those who cultivate the full human relationship to Nature, as it is, without a rigid insistence on particular approaches, are 'yogis' and true 'Taoists,' regardless of what they may call themselves. Such cultivation depends not on dogmas but on a direct and balanced perception of how livingness operates, how chi patterns itself.

Whatever else is included in this vision (depending on individual personal affinities), it must encompass *humanness*, without distortion, and without prejudicing our view of Nature by clinging to the usual limitations we tend to impose on human experience. The exercise of this perception of our participation in Nature's patterns is 'yoga.'

Thus, given a freedom from pretense and a clear view of how we interact with Nature, we may proceed with the yogic process of *celebrating* that relationship. This process in turn further enriches the relationship.

At some point in our experience of SEVEN, an irresistible urge arose to see and enjoy this openness in a more determinate way. We then instinctively reached out to 'touch' the infinite possibilities implicit at SEVEN, making them and their ordering patterns explicit (thus EIGHT).

This gesture is another way of explaining the awakening to Eight, and emphasizes that, along with the basic principles revealed at EIGHT, the fundamental patterns of energy that constitute our connection with Nature are also exposed. These patterns are the so-called "yogic channels."

Usually misunderstood as tubes running through the body, the channels are actually repeating patterns of energy spanning the personal and universal domains. Such fundamental patterns 'magnetize' or attract the occurrence of more such patterns, essentially "commanding a following," which is why fleshed-out forms arise in Nature and also why we speak of 'laws' at EIGHT. But here the apparent boundary between us and Nature resulting from such delineated forms is not in evidence—only the basic patterns themselves are at issue.

We have stopped focussing on the atmosphere of our personal environment, and notice instead the patterns or channels connecting that atmosphere to the rest of the universe. These channels render us sensitive to the many dimensions of Nature. Also, such channels actually constitute, by the shapes of their patterned movement, the structure of Nature.

All this becomes available to us when the body, formed of these channels, is activated by a basic urge founded in the openness of SEVEN. This urge to enter EIGHT—and the rest of the Way—is very primordial desire, naked and unrestrained. Such a desire to *use* our embodied nature as the basis for appreciating Nature isn't precisely comparable to the ordinary desire to 'use' something or to make something happen. Nevertheless, it is in fact an important part of what all desire, beginning in ONE, really involves.

Just as a hungry Monkey in his tree would reach out to grab fruit, there is a natural longing and reaching out in the process of transition from SEVEN to EIGHT. We could never say that it was wrong for Monkey to leap around his tree, searching for fruit, grabbing everything that caught his eye. That was his nature, ultimately founded on the natural longing and understanding of a much more potent way of 'reaching out,' more fully revealed in our passage to EIGHT.

Nature's movements are subtle here, but run through all phenomena ... Yin still separates from Yang, "coming and going" occur simultaneously, in everything. The urge toward union asserts itself in a primordial fashion, without exhausting itself in some final state or goal. This urge is the ground of both sexual attraction in Nature and of those yogic practices which express the completion inherent in that attraction.

It's impossible to compare the strength or focus of this urge with any ordinary desires. While it represents the perfection of Monkey's desire nature, no Monkey remains to distort it, nor does the 'civilized' veneer of Sage remain to inhibit it. Lacking the usual restrictions and preoccupations with objects and goals, it is so direct it's actually 'desireless.'

This is no longer the action of an individual person, but is SEVEN itself, in some general sense, reaching out to EIGHT. No man or woman needs any training in acting from this urge.

There is instant mastery without instruction, free experimentation without ignorance. When we reach out with this natural intention, we essentially "lay our hands" directly on the Five Elements themselves.

Having made that connection, we may then go on, at NINE, to practice the yoga of being "at Source," experimenting with embodying a kind of 'procreative' principle of manifestation. This will become possible in NINE because the yogic channels are unobstructed by a small view. They complete our connections to the full play of Yin and Yang and the Five Elements, and through them the Originating Energy of the Source can manifest.

AWAKENING TO THE SYMPHONY OF NATURE

At EIGHT neighboring NINE, we are much less tentative in our cultivation of the Way, much more willing to leave the sideline and move to the center. We're finally emerging from the shyness of SEVEN, where we were absorbed in the quietude and equanimity of inaction.

We might describe this as a growing response to the music of Nature. When we first realized that the fullness and complexity of EIGHT's 'sound' did not really disturb SEVEN's equanimity, we relaxed and permitted—even sought out—exposure to Nature's symphony.

We witnessed Great Order, listening to its tune of all things "coming into being and reaching completion." Finally, we became empowered to enjoy our basic participation in this symphonic process as members of a great and diverse community of living beings, all Cultivators of the Way.

We can now go on, in NINE, to appreciate Nature's music even better, 'seeing' precisely how our familiar world and its events contribute to the symphony. Beyond that, in TEN, we will also become inspired to add our own individual human voices to the music.

At NINE, the universal principles of Nature are dressed in the garments of natural phenomena, appearing in a pristine state without the imposition of value judgments. The manifest world is thus reborn without having undergone a death, transformed without having ever really changed, resting vibrantly in primordial paradox.

NINE

SECTION I: RETURNING FROM NOWHERE

NINE is shown as a star-filled, luminous sky above mountains and cliffs overlooking the waves lapping on a seashore.

NINE's Image depicts the entire manifest face of Nature as *conspicuously* participating in a joyous Cultivation of the Way.

The Image shows moon and stars shining in the newly sun-lit sky, representing a balance of Yin and Yang energies, but with Yang ascending. This indicates that, at NINE, Cultivating the Way is becoming more active and definite, in contrast to the vast but somewhat passive, general appreciation characterizing SEVEN and EIGHT.

The luminous quality of NINE's Image reminds us that light is now abundantly present, and this light reveals our surroundings and context. In all such revelations and encounters, we still tend to perceive what is familiar or suited to us. So here, familiar physical form is again manifest, everywhere.

THE RETURN OF THE PHYSICAL

In NINE, definite forms and 'the physical' have returned, expressing both the openness of SEVEN and the raw principles of EIGHT. It's as though alluring garments and other finery have slipped down over the undifferentiated plainness of SEVEN and the stark skeletal

133

patterns seen in EIGHT, offering a more accessible and human view of Nature.

This isn't a matter of *covering up* Nature. Rather, NINE shows that form and physicality constitute another fundamental phase of Nature's energy, a phase that Taoists feel is particularly important to understand. Physical form is essentially elaborate energy patterning, following and developing the themes of EIGHT.

The 'channels' which provide the framework for the 'emergence' of the universe at NINE might be thought of as the habit patterns available in the universe to become primary human experience. A cultivator at NINE simply singles out and follows the patterns appropriate to his nature.

Actually, this is the mechanism by which everything always manifests. At NINE, it's simply seen directly and explored in an intimate fashion, permitting us to verify our connection with Nature. In ONE through SIX, we alternately disregarded and became obsessed by this patterned, brocade quality overlaying openness and basic principle. But now, at NINE, physical form beautifully expresses these dimensions of Nature.

What returns at NINE is not our own individual physicality, nor the prosaic physicalness people (in ONE through FIVE) normally take for granted and unconsciously associate with objects of perception. Rather, it's physicalness *as it actually is*—represented by the world itself. "The world" considered by Monkey and Sage was just a toy version.

NINE is the point at which we "encounter the world," directly and truly. We connect to the real nature of its concreteness and presence, far more than we ever could by distractedly knocking about as "independent subjects" in the world of ONE through SIX.

"NATURE IMAGERY" IN TAOISM

The Image of NINE emphasizes the familiar world of sun, moon, mountains, and oceans, in particular, because they are the traditional objects of most Taoist cultivators' attention. However, Taoism's preference for such Nature imagery has seldom been understood.

Taoists living in remote areas are not romanticizing Nature or extolling the virtues of primitive living. They're intently cultivating an appreciation of NINE by focussing on the most potent, manifestly physical things in the universe ... in essence, they're testing their view in the most stringent way possible. Traditional Chinese arts such as landscape painting were also originally inspired by and express NINE's view of Nature.

Human beings and their affairs are all too easily seen as evanescent, ephemeral. By contrast, oceans and mountains usually seem timeless to us, and so it's very difficult for us to see them as being *phases*. For this very reason, if we can look at a mountain and see it as a veil giving shape to chaos, or as a particular concrete phase of energy which leaves energy's open dimensions still hovering and available, then we have truly understood physicalness.

The point is not simply to see a mountain, for example, as being *transitory*. It is also a phase in a very different and more important sense—it's a particular manifestation of energies which are also connected to energy movements proceeding in other ways, at various rates, forward and backward in time, through all possible creative and destructive cycles.

A mountain is actually the 'confluence' or presence of all these possibilities. Only a few of them are usually of interest to human beings, but many may be of central interest to the other types of beings sharing the living universe with us. A Cultivator of the Way is committed to exploring and cultivating his own human relationship to Nature, but an appreciation of other possibilities and of how such relationships work, in general, is also useful.

Our world and those of various other beings alluded to in traditional Taoist cosmology are really one and the same multi-faceted world. Moreover, because all physical bodies, *including our own*, have so many aspects, they're connection points to the entire universe and to all the various facets of Nature Itself. Our energy channels are paths to everywhere, and traversing such paths actually *forms* what we find.

135

Yogic cultivators of the Way have long understood, like Lao Tzu in the more philosophical tradition, that Nature is not so much a particular characterizable thing but a generous response to our own needs and advances toward It. Moreover, even these approaches and responses are founded in the Stages themselves. This is the subject of the next Section.

NINE

SECTION II: A MATTER OF PERSPECTIVE

NINE throws new 'light' on both the openness of physical things and on the responsive, mutually-revealing character of our relationships to Nature. The basic issue is our own role as observers in shaping the reality manifest at various stages of the Way.

SEVEN, EIGHT, and NINE view the same Space with different perspectives, and with different intensities resulting from various types of *intimacy* with our context. At NINE, we can look back to SEVEN and EIGHT, and see several important aspects of this intimacy.

SEVEN definitively showed that nothing exists in the old way that Monkey and Sage took for granted. Moreover, during the cultivator's initial passage into SEVEN, nothing is familiar enough to "be anything" in any other, newer way. So we see little, and anything that *is* apparent is rather uncharacterized. Compared to the definiteness of the self-image and its situations in ONE through SIX, at SEVEN there might seem to be no events and no observer-observed relationship left.

However, if we continue with a calm assessment and acceptance of this apparently blank place (SEVEN), we sense—without seeing—a lot of activity, the movement of *chi*-energy on a hitherto unimagined scale. At a certain point, this comes to suggest *phenomena*, rather than just threatening more chaos. The movement hints that "something's happening" (in the supposedly empty space), and this new

137

type of movement is also subtly *linked* to the chaos rather than standing as an exception to it. So in a sense, the chaos suggests order.

We're starting to glimpse the fact that both chaos and order are fundamental to the real movements of Nature. Movement isn't restricted to being just the predictable patterns of ONE through SIX. Nor must the alternative be *only* absolute chaos going in all directions. Thus, as we experience Nature more clearly and broadly, we become less vulnerable to an intoxication induced either by pervasive chaos or the monotonous hum of order.

At EIGHT and NINE, movement can be seen to run naturally between chaos and order. *In the same way, both life and the Way necessarily run between chaos and order.* The interdependence between chaos and order also eliminates any residual notions of 'knowledge' or 'truth' as being fixed and definite.

The intimate and active relationship between the cultivator and his context is far more open than ordinary subject-object interactions. It too involves a connection between chaos and order, and this connection is inherent even in the relationships between the Stages.

THE STAGES AS VANTAGE POINTS

In our first pass through SEVEN, we had 'lost' the vantage points of Monkey, Sage, and Mountain. However, just because our vantage point was without characteristic doesn't mean there was no vantage point left, or that vantage points are inappropriate. 'We' initially viewed SEVEN with a perceptual set subtly tinged by a sense of order, a residue of our experience in ONE through SIX. Compared to our lingering taste for order, SEVEN then looked empty or chaotic.

As we became more comfortable in SEVEN, we accepted it. In the process, we found true Chaos, something entirely open and unrestricted, rather than being merely chaotic in the sense of being strange to us. And in our acceptance of Chaos, we thereby *assumed* that position in our opening to the rest of Nature. We actually became the Chaos at the heart of SEVEN!

From there, things again look different ... Chaos posits order, so EIGHT's Great Order emerges in response to our living at the heart of SEVEN. The more we become Chaos, the more clearly EIGHT appears.

So, in a sense, EIGHT is something seen by SEVEN. When EIGHT fills our view, we *are* the position of SEVEN, the "vantage point" of real Chaos, enticing the real Order of EIGHT to emerge. Compared to EIGHT, the order characterizing ONE through SIX is entirely incoherent, discordant, because its true context and scope haven't yet been found.

This tentative courtship sparks a further, more definite urge toward union with EIGHT's Order. As 'we' (Chaos) press forward, continuing to make advances, Order naturally dresses up for us, using the familiar and alluring imagery so characteristic of NINE.

Since SEVEN, the Way has proceeded much more clearly through this mutually-defining dance. It's a movement which is both too powerful and too delicate to be made by Monkey and Sage, too responsive to be managed by the old, rather inert sense of body.

So as we said, the interaction of the Stages themselves really constitutes the unfolding of the Way. It's not a matter of producing or achieving the Stages. The Stages *are* fundamental aspects of Nature (for human beings) ... as such, they coexist and operate in their characteristic ways, but they're also defined by the movement or Way which links them to one another.

MANIFESTATIONS' ORDER AND FREEDOM

At NINE, we connect to that aspect of ourselves which is big enough to incite the Universe to come forward to meet us. As the Image suggests, at NINE the waves of the entire world of form lap on the shore of the human experience. 'Our' increasing potency as Chaos and our proximity to Order decorates it, usually drawing on familiar human themes (like the ocean, mountain, etc.). But in fact, the possibilities of what Chaos would require of Order are infinitely diverse—they are absolutely everything that exists in Nature.

So, the cultivator as Chaos may choose the very primordial earthly imagery of ocean, moon, and stars. But as a cultivator grows more free in his role as Chaos and wishes to actively explore his nature by experimenting in that role, Order may appear in many guises, depending on the cultivator's energy connections and approach.

Nature may appear as a beautiful lover, or as a 'god' or a bull-headed demon—whatever Order looks like to the type of Chaos approaching it. For example, NINE is the place where we can put definite faces on the entitative aspect of Nature. We then explore a variety of interactions with other types of beings who already enjoy the freedom of their relationship with Nature and may support our own cultivation of the Way.

When I was studying in Taiwan, my teachers determined that my nature was particularly given to practices based on relationships with such helpful intermediaries (as aspects of Nature). I was therefore encouraged to 'approach' a particular, very important 'protector' of my teachers' lineage, and was told in great detail how this protector appeared. But, in fact, when my 'call' was heard, the protector who responded appeared in a very different and far more prepossessing form.

After I reviewed my experience with my teachers, they explained that the form I saw was of the same protector, but was considered typical of a much earlier period of Taoist practice and was rarely seen in modern times. I can't go into details here about this, except to make the essential point that this encounter was the result of a selection process based on a relationship involving *both* my own affinities and also the possible range of forms associated with the entity I sought. The entity—like all other parts of the luminous environment—does not appear randomly, but rather presents one of a specific set of different faces to a particular cultivator, depending on his nature. Such presentations and experiences are the result of an interaction between the nature of our personal environment (shen) and the luminous Tao.

Of course, when we talk about a cultivator's individual characteristics and affinities here, we're not talking about someone's *personality*. The perceiver pole is rather undifferentiated at NINE. But there is still some vestige of an individual character (observer) here, because even though we've dissolved into this enormity of Chaos, the Chaos itself remains, in a whimsical, individual fashion, a viewpoint.

This 'individual' Chaos has great latitude in pursuing its courtship—it is not hampered by our old identifications and preferences. We don't need to retrieve our small notion of who or what we are in order to follow the Way. We're now openness and Chaos on a scale that is both usable and utterly unimaginable. All the obstacles, confusions and expectations of human beings, as they typically live, are just specks of dust in the huge process that we participate in at NINE.

FACETS OF DESIRE IN CULTIVATING THE WAY

There are no petty personal problems, habits, or obsessions operating at NINE. But the essential quality of our urge toward an opposite or complement, and our confusion (deriving from the dual, polarized character of the Way) still persist.

The basic quality of our agitation, urges and confusion as Monkey and Sage, are all revealed here as being natural and fundamental, not to be rejected. We have willingly become real Confusion, real Problem now! Even *these* tensions are genuine features of the living Way, and must actually be respected as part of the fruit of cultivation.

At the mountain peak in SIX, Monkey and Sage reached through to a glimpse of this point—they realized that they hadn't gotten any better, and this is why they were so humbled by the view from the mountain. In fact, they'd begun to see clearly that what lies ahead, in SEVEN and beyond, is real Problem, the ultimate defeat of their agendas. Only when they really gave up did their true natures become available to the force leading to SEVEN.

The force that Monkey and Sage finally yield to at SIX is thus, in a sense, not a newly-created 'power.' It's a trust and acceptance of this reciprocal, impossible to pin down, urge between Order and Chaos, moving into a Space large enough to give it free rein for its play.

Monkey is (relatively) chaos while Sage is order, but both are rather limited 'takes' on these principles. Comparatively speaking, both are still on the 'order' side, needing a broader base as chaos before further Wayfaring is possible.

So, Monkey, Sage and the mountain lose their initial ordered and definite forms to their nature as an openness or Chaos. Chaos, in turn, takes on another, Ordered aspect, assuming whatever forms are beautiful or attractive to itself. *For, Order is where Chaos must go to circulate, to fulfill itself.*

As we'll see in TEN, we can go on to *become* the Order pole again. When we do so, we view Chaos (the energy to potentiate anything) as that which runs through us and inspires us.

These same principles are involved in subtleties like the polar character of all ordinary perception and in the more overt aspects of interpersonal or sexual attraction operating in life. The tug-of-war and mutual attractions linking Monkey and Sage are also related to these dynamics, revealed fully at NINE, enjoyed well into TEN, and resolved (not denied) at ELEVEN and TWELVE. But the Way to TWELVE is really a return to a tolerant, encompassing fullness, embracing all the possible human relationships to Nature.

SELF RESPECT AND "PROPER CONDUCT"

There are no lowly or evil desires, but only weird hats and odd masks for various natural urges. The entire Way is natural. It is what it needs to be, and is characterized by alternating phases, not by evolution toward something better.

We have a tendency to forget this when we're caught in the conflicts deriving from our engagement in some activity that is supposedly unworthy or 'bad.' But if we really look into the naked quality of our desire, we can decide the issue properly.

Our motivation may be to approach something we truly want and need at some level. So our excursions into such territory are not necessarily departures from the Way. However, if we misapprehend the situation by rigidly clinging to a small view regarding ourselves or the true object of our desire, then we can become distracted and enmeshed in an 'evil' battle with ourselves or others, creating harm.

As long as we keep our desires in perspective, grounding them in our basic character and that of the Way, then regardless of how idiosyncratic or untraditional our preferred activity may be at times, we're instantly right in the middle of the living—rather than idealized—understanding of the Way. We therefore enjoy the same direct access to the Way's supporting energy that is supposed to be provided by traditional yogic practices and prescribed codes of conduct.

The same point applies to the 'indulgence' of our various character traits. For example, Taoism particularly differs from some other traditions on the issue of laziness. Some people see laziness as one of the main obstacles in meditation, and recommend, as a standard "patent remedy," the exercise of exceptional vigilance and efforts toward the goal of transcendence of all such limitations. Taoist cultivators also find this energy of laziness, but simply tap into its naked character and include it in their practice, thereby effortlessly exposing a more encompassing appreciation of the Way.

Hacking at one's nature with judgments and a "fix it" mentality is not cultivating the Way. It will only exhaust us, and if that should happen it's certainly not a "higher state," despite sensations of transcendence. If we stick to the themes of SEVEN, EIGHT, and NINE, we will avoid futile struggles and concocted realizations. Acceptance of ourselves creates the short path of cultivation, founded in the existing momentum of the human relationship to Nature. So if we truly accept our 'laziness,' this is a very powerful gesture of cultivation and trust in Nature.

We can live in the flirtatious quality of polarity and in all our ups and downs, playing with them in real but very open-ended situations, without worrying about which parts we and our situation might have at a given time—Chaos or Order. This is actually looking ahead a bit, to TEN, but the point must take hold and grow in NINE. We and the world—without selective picking and choosing—participate in major, universally 'liberating' movements of energy, and this is the basis for true cultivation. With this enlarged view of conduct and liberating action, we enter into NINE's most centrally yogic role—union.

NINE

SECTION III: YOGA AND ORIGINATING ENERGY

NINE is shown as a star-filled, luminous sky above mountains and cliffs overlooking the waves lapping on a seashore. The Image depicts the subtle movement and power of Nature, as well as the continuous transformations of its forms.

We repeat the root text on NINE's Image to consider another of its main points. As the Image shows, Heavenly factors (the primordial 'stars' figuring in astrology) and more conventional agents (ordinary stars, weather, plants, etc.) joyously intermingle.

Form has 'returned' or become apparent again, but so have its connections with the influences of Nature. Even when not directly 'seen,' these influences are clearly felt by the cultivator at NINE. We are now sensitive to the energy dimensions through which these forces operate to regulate all earthly processes (just as the moon in the Image would affect the ocean's tides).

The subtle and rather general principles of EIGHT are now depicted as Heavenly bodies. They act upon us and our world in lawlike ways, currents arising from EIGHT's Great Order.

Such forces have innumerable consequences, but are not limited to their effects, nor to being things or events in space or time. They have no substance or 'strength,' but yet hold sway. These forces' action is on-going and connects our world to the living center or Source.

144

Rather than being 'causes' whose action is completed in the past, they leave the returning world itself rather magical. It is highly patterned and clearly revealed, yet not fixed in character ... it could still become anything, since it enjoys a living relationship with Nature.

We've already seen that, depending on how we experience Nature, we can describe both its forces and their creations very differently. Nature may seem 'cosmic' and impersonal. Or the characteristic affinities and dynamics of our approach may put particular faces on some factors, thus casting them in more entitative guises—gods, angels, demons, unusual friends. At NINE, both possibilities are relevant and well-grounded, and in fact are only two of many possible views.

Whatever approach we take, the efficacy of our connecting to such forces derives from our willingness and ability to embrace Nature in a fully human way, without unnecessary reservations. This understanding sets NINE in strong contrast to the early Stages.

In ONE through FIVE, Monkey and Sage saw Nature as an enemy, or a necessary but rather irrelevant environment, or perhaps as remote and all-powerful, victimizing us without even caring. Both Monkey and Sage dreamed of dominating Nature, acting as a sorcerer, a scientist, or a civilized gentleman who had risen above the "exigencies of the wilderness." Their approaches limited Nature's replies, and ruled out an active and complete relationship.

In fact, our relationship to Nature is much more than could ever be encompassed by neurotic notions like 'command,' 'dependency,' or 'independence.' Being a sorcerer, victim, or gentleman are not the only possibilities. At NINE, we realize that our connections with Nature are already so vast in number and kind that we need no longer assume any *limiting* separation between "us and It."

Originating Energy is represented here as the influence of Heavenly Bodies on the phenomenal World.

As we become more accustomed to NINE, we become increasingly familiar with the operation of the Originating Energy (tien chi) manifesting and nurturing all things. But we sensed from the outset

145

that the "creation of the world" is a cooperative matter. Our 'contribution' as observers is subtly felt in the emerging forms, and the implications of this sensed participation become more apparent as NINE unfolds.

First, we've seen that Nature's creative impulse is channeled by the fundamental human patterns which are invoked when we accept our identity with Chaos. We are essentially *human Chaos* driving Order to dress up for us. In entering NINE, we thus receive a practical education in the application of Great Order to our world. In addition, we begin to realize that Nature's creative role is not really *external* to us.

As more patterns or channels are traced out in Nature, as more of the world returns, and as our own participation is more acutely felt, an urge arises to join in even more intimately with this creative process. We acknowledge our unity with both manifest Nature and Nature's creative womb.

This is a delicate and important turning point within NINE. It's the stage where we begin to investigate the possibility of *being and acting* as the creative center of Nature Itself.

In such experimentation, our understanding is not absolute ... we may 'succeed' or 'fail,' guess correctly or not. In either case, the experimental process deepens our appreciation of Nature's Way.

This urge to experiment with "manifesting the universe" is not at all a matter of sorcery, of seeking personal power. It's simply an expression of the intention, grounded in direct experience and honest testing, to look into and exercise our *full* human relationship to Nature. Again, in this exercise, there must be no prejudices or arbitrary limits placed on what that relationship might encompass. So the cultivator at NINE may play with physical manifestation, making and unmaking, changing things in as many ways as possible to test his understanding.

At first, we aren't really concerned with exactly who we are in this activity, just that these profound possibilities are within reach and inform our cultivation of the Way. It feels natural for us to explore them.

In doing so, however, we don't end up particularly powerful or skill-ful, nor have we learned any magic tricks ... we simply become our-selves. This is the real point of Taoism.

We discover that these possibilities only look extraordinary because we're making an explicit exercise of them. They seem like special cases initially, but basically they're just reflections of the scope of ordi-nary natural process.

Eventually, we drop the special effort of the exercise, but life con-tinues to operate and so the true profundity remains, clearly revealed. It's just a matter of doing something and realizing that *doing it is who and what we are* as living human beings.

With this acknowledgment, we spontaneously re-emerge in the world, fully formed and functional, as immortal at TEN. Our true nature, which expressed an unstoppable, rather *erotic* interest in Great Order at EIGHT and in concrete form at NINE, is now moving into action, intensely intimate but entirely ordinary action ... the yogic action of living in the world, day by day.

Our nature has found itself in a context large enough to be true to life—without any developmental process or by moving from igno-rance to an accumulated knowledge, just by accepting its joy in participating in Nature. In TEN, this joy will be expressed in very simple and personal ways, but with unprecedented freedom.

TEN is a spontaneous dance with the energy and circumstances of our surroundings, a personal celebration of the
basic dynamics of Nature.

TEN

SECTION I: THE EARTHLY HSIEN

At TEN, we are engaged in completely active forms of cultivation, proceeding within a thoroughly open, multi-dimensional Time.

At TEN, the Earthly Immortal (Hsien) emerges fully mature, dancing in response to the currents of Earthly energy that surround him.

The Chinese character for 'hsien' (Immortal) is a composite of the characters for 'man' and 'mountain.' In TEN's Image, the human cultivator is back, acting on the same mountain peak as in SIX, but with a much-expanded view of that situation.

The process that 'restored' the world at NINE now brings forward the cultivator's form at TEN ... the human body is here experienced to be a pattern woven of component patterns of energy. So the usual processes of manifestation are still operating, and it is these, not something arcane or unnatural, that have brought us back again in Immortal form, without any special effort.

The human relationship to Nature here is much like that of a hawk floating on the wind or of a fish swimming through the currents of a stream. It's our basic human nature functioning in Nature, expressing itself in its essential physicality and sensitivity. The Hsien is naturally being "made alive" by Nature.

"CULTIVATING IMMORTALITY"

TEN is about immortality, and those who experience it are traditionally called 'hsien.' The real meaning of cultivating immortality is at the heart of the human relationship to Nature.

At NINE, the more manifest aspect of Nature returns to demonstrate that physicality is quite real, but real in a way that's not appreciated until it's put in perspective—seen as a specific phase of energies following the cue of the fundamental patterns of EIGHT and registering on the cultivator. This inspires us to experiment with 'manifestation,' and culminates in the manifestation of ourselves and the immortality of our own existence at TEN.

Such experiments are not random tinkering, and the investigation of immortality is not merely a last experiment—it exposes the essence of what is actually alive and running through all manifestations, through all of Nature.

At TEN, therefore, we've closed the circle, finding ourselves in the full context of Nature. So too, the Earthly Hsien emerges fully mature, indicating that he and his immortality aren't *produced*.

We haven't necessarily become something extraordinary or 'achieved' indefinitely prolonged lives. But we have exposed the full, on-going human relationship to Nature, and now proceed to enjoy it.

The scope of that relationship is so vast and potent that it affords us an 'immortal' experience of the universe. However, what is the *motive* behind that experience?

MOTIVES

When we experienced ourselves as Monkey and Sage, desire for gain was the outward *face* of the only motive available for a while, and it sufficed to get us to SIX's peak ... Monkey and Sage both needed some incentive of this sort to justify their partnership. (Of course, for Sage it masqueraded under various altruistic masks until SIX.) But a desire to gain from a relationship is not a motive that could possibly take us to TEN.

The movement to TEN is strictly a natural attraction for what is under all those masks and early misapprehensions of ourselves. We haven't particularly *benefitted* from bringing forward the immortal perspective, nor have we striven for anything unnatural. We've simply sought, found, and live in what is true!

Undoubtedly, in all periods of history some people have become preoccupied with attaining 'immortality' in the petty sense of prolonging their bodies, their personalities, etc. Such pursuits were particularly prominent among those who wished to make their fortunes in the old imperial courts of power, where personal longevity was inevitably sought at any price. And it is these pursuits that tend to have been recorded and remain available for study by scholars. More generally, some "taoist yoga" has been rather fanciful or carried to outlandish lengths at times.

These are all cases in which the natural dynamic of the Way at a mature stage, in this case TEN, is echoed in toy practices or agendas at FOUR or FIVE, where Monkey and Sage still prevail. It's important to note the difference. A history of obsessive behavior by people at FIVE doesn't deny the possibility of cultivators in later Stages practicing cultivation in a way that's more natural, well-founded, and generally relevant.

Monkey and Sage as such don't *create* the important themes—'cultivation,' 'immortality,' etc. Those come from the dynamics revealed in SEVEN through TEN as operating in all of us, not from the mimicry and self-seeking of ONE through SIX.

The traditional yogic agenda of Taoism has been to experiment for a very simple purpose. From SEVEN through NINE, we may apply yoga to accumulate or vitalize our energy, and to nurture our bodies. We may also play with Nature and its manifestations, possibly varying and redirecting its patterns in uncommon ways. Such 'cultivation' is done, *not* to improve or extend our lives or increase our power, but to *concentrate*—and thereby *clarify*—what we are, to completely experience what our relationship with Nature really is. That's all!

This type of vigorous experimentation and cultivation is essential, and can be generally recommended to all cultivators. For, precisely because the shen is an essential *summary* of what we really are, we must activate and apply ourselves sufficiently to experience the fullness of life and its essential oneness with the Tao (Nature).

The point is to have a complete experience of humanness. *We thus connect to the life we are in,* and seek only to do that.

Acting without concern for self-preservation or any pre-defined agenda, but from a boundless desire to participate in life fully, as it is, the cultivator experiments to appreciate the human relationship to Nature. The Earthly Immortal embodies the resulting discovery that, taken together and in perspective, the things that are *real* about the universe have no death in them. He also sees that we participate, centrally and in a very human way, in those realities.

So there's no clinging involved, no concern about either fixing ourselves or making "what we really are" immune to Nature. Such concerns are unnecessary, and the latter in particular would indeed be a travesty.

Cultivation without pretence, including all that we actually find ourselves to be, without embarrassment, bonding with our situation rather than trying to leave or improve ... these have been the watchwords of the Way from the beginning. We started in ONE and TWO with what we *appear* to be—Monkey and Sage, on various levels and in various ways. Those were the closest approximations we were then capable of making. And we took them as far as we could.

In SEVEN we found what was not fundamental about them, dropping the toys and frivolous decorative items for a plain acknowledgment of our bare, essential character. In EIGHT and NINE, we went on to find what was true about us in a positive sense.

When we became sufficiently accustomed to openness, Great Order, and manifestation's link to both, so we could let it all apply to ourselves, then automatically we and the world *both* returned as the very human situation of TEN. The Earthly Immortal's entire existence is inseparable from the activity of the world at large, and he freely demonstrates that situation as involving a Way which *all our lives* are following.

ASPECTS OF IMMORTALITY

Everyone has moments where they relax into or accept their lives and thereby enjoy the Earthly Hsien's view to some extent ... in those instants they grasp the Hsien's 'immortality.' At TEN this view is simply more stable and fully fleshed out, more applicable.

TEN shows the entire "human relationship to Nature" concretely and continuously, as it applies to us *individually*. But this relationship is too encompassing to justify notions of separate 'things' in relation to one another, so the sense of human isolation in the universe is completely dispelled. We are not 'mortal' in the tragic and problematical sense, because we're not cut off, left to wither while elsewhere "life goes on."

We are entirely hooked up with Nature. Our channels have all been brought into active awareness and are connected to every facet of the multi-dimensional universe—there's no loose ends or dangling hoses, and we are not just some needy or parasitic organisms drawing on Nature's generosity from one end of the hoses.

The nurturing and transformative processes which we really *are* include 'life' and 'death,' and are about 'living' in a larger sense. They are the respiratory phases and circulation of the entire living universe. After SEVEN, EIGHT, and NINE, we've *become* the open-ended Center, the Order, and both the forms and the formative energies of that universe.

The particular values of our body-energy states come and go, but the shen—the summary and significance of our nature as Nature in its various aspects—is neither ephemeral nor eternal. Both ideas are too limiting to describe Nature, and thus also fail to describe us.

The shen is not an immortal soul but a part of the open, multi-dimensional field of Nature, and that suffices to ground 'immortality.' Since 'we' and Nature are ONE through SIX, mortality is a natural part of the picture. But since 'we' and Nature are also SEVEN, EIGHT, and NINE, 'immortality' characterizes our situation in several different ways, all showing that duration and its opposite do not measure our livingness.

Our release from preoccupations with mortality had actually already begun at SEVEN. SEVEN does show immortality, since it emphasizes a freedom from processes and events ... also, to the extent that something is happening in SEVEN, it 'goes' in all directions and is thus not limited to being a process of decay.

EIGHT continues this education, revealing an Order beyond conflict, and so resolves the tragedy apparently involved in death. We see transformative processes in a new light.

NINE and TEN make the same point in more specific ways. We see the background against which manifestation occurs, and the overlapping types of time and energy which leave all manifestations quite open-ended, not trapped in fixed identities and degenerative spirals. We also see that we can use our channels' connections to Nature to draw all the sustenance we need, even to stay young if we wish. But the purpose of exploring the latter possibility is *to know our connectedness fully,* not necessarily to *exploit* it for longevity once the basic point has been made.

So we play with the possibilities of mortality and immortality, studying our situation. Perhaps it's true that an immortal physical form is impossible in a sense, maybe even a contradiction in terms. But the cultivator can find ways around the impossibility, ways founded in his connection to Nature. Nevertheless, indefinite prolongation of life is not the real issue, and because it's not the issue we allow it to fail at some point, submitting ourselves to naturally benign transformative processes.

The body can indeed be made "immortal for a while," but only to understand the much larger sense of immortality pertaining to the life we are in. Our essential nature exists, not in the ordinary time of ONE through SIX, but in the living time glimpsed at SEVEN and fully revealed at TEN. This is the time of "no death," of true immortality.

Each of us must learn how we participate in that time, and there is no trick or general formula which addresses that point. The 'tricks' people have developed over the centuries have never worked reliably, of course, because immortality is a very delicate and individual matter. Immortality is relevant to cultivation precisely because it's about who each of us is, living in the Tao.

Modern scholars of Chinese history have sometimes expressed amusement at the credulity of followers who believed in a master's attainment of immortality even after he manifestly had died. But in fact the issue is not so simple, nor the "belief in immortality" so simplistic or narrowly motivated.

WORLDLY KNOWLEDGE

The "cultivation of immortality" may seem like a strictly "worldly concern," deriving from a rather worldly knowledge or wisdom. But that is true in a way that's quite profound. The real agenda *is* to stay with Nature, *not* to somehow transcend it.

The central issue is indeed the human relationship to Nature. It's all that we have, all we will ever have.

Attempts to transcend Nature just "jump the track" of reality. They stray into concocted realizations or—at best—special experiences which unconsciously use our nature and connection to the universe.

Special or transcendent experiences of some aspect of our nature— no matter how extraordinary—are not the heart of the matter. Reporting such experiences, without putting them in the larger context of the Way, and claiming them to be the "way out" of our situation, is inappropriate.

There's no way to leave what we are, and no need to do so. The Earthly Hsien is—as the name suggests—the embodiment of a final accommodation with the world, and in that sense does represent a worldly view. But there is plenty of scope in that view for grounding and potentiating even the highest forms of cultivating the Way.

TEN

SECTION II: THE DANCE OF LIFE

The view available to the Earthly Hsien empowers and galvanizes us. EIGHT emphasized the principles of union with Nature, and NINE the application of that process in formative terms. At TEN a 'skin' is laid over the process, and the true cultivator of the Way appears as the Earthly Hsien. The Earthly Hsien's activity is not a specific collection of exertions, but the life expressed by EIGHT and NINE, embodied at TEN.

The Earthly Hsien is really back in the world. Rather than focussing on universals, he's entering into the action which he *is* and which is happening everywhere. This is his cultivation—his action, his life.

Thinking is not the issue at TEN ... the cultivator enters completely into pure action. So TEN's Image shows the Immortal in a pose associated with the movements of ritual dance. These derive from the ancient shamanic origins of Taoism and demonstrate the energy and movement of EIGHT and NINE.

The Immortal is back at the mountain top of SIX to stand in contrast with more ordinary approaches to cultivation, which also reached their pinnacle there. The efforts of FIVE, that previously appeared to dominate and determine the course of the Way, are clearly shown to have a limited scope. For, whereas Monkey and Sage faced their end at the peak, the Immortal is the true nature of what they were and is not caught in their dilemma ... he can *descend* the mountain, and in a

157

way that continues the activity of cultivation rather than being an admission of failure. The reality of ONE through NINE goes with him. Nothing has been left behind.

Activity in the world offers the Earthly Hsien enormous scope for cultivation. And if he should want to do 'meditation' now, he essentially becomes EIGHT or NINE, as required, tuning in to Great Order and manifestation in the world. No artificial techniques by a 'doer' are involved in cultivation, only various styles of 'dancing,' reflecting the Stages' interpenetration. It's true that dancing could be accomplished by learning steps and technique, but at TEN we just "join in with the beat" of life and Nature.

CRITIQUES OF ARTIFICE IN CULTIVATION

In ancient times, a growing preoccupation with artifice and rigid, obsessive notions of cultivation motivated the critiques of technical yogic practice made by Chuang Tzu, perhaps even earlier by Lao Tzu. It's sometimes said that they were "anti-yoga," but this overlooks the possibility that they were recommending (as we have done) a proper view or perspective on what yogic experimentation is, and how and to what extent a cultivator needs to practice it. Chuang Tzu in particular was urging people not to make an obstacle of technique, and to feel free to abandon it, in the sense that we should abandon all pretence and unnaturalness. Our own individual nature is the Way, and TEN sees and relies upon it.

TEN liberates all preoccupation with technique, precision, and expertise. Even in NINE, which also enjoyed a correct (natural) view of cultivation and was not tainted by the small-minded tinkering of FIVE, there could still be a meticulous quality to yoga and experimentation, a sense that we were exploring visions and must be very precise about what they represent, how they work, etc. Action in NINE was correspondingly very careful, followed like a scripted thing.

In TEN we trust that everything arising is fine as it is. We inhabit the essence of all manifestation and our spontaneity becomes one with Great Order.

People often think that as we move further into the Way, we must get 'better' at it and that as a result cultivation speeds up. It's true that in earlier Stages, as we cooperated more with ourselves, life seemed to be facilitated, to jump ahead at times. But this is not the kind of efficiency we enjoy now.

At TEN, things simply are as they are. We exist in time as something we're immersed in—the past, present, and future are all there, and little time bubbles rise up and pop before our faces as the events of our lives, the joys and releases, etc. And though this way of living is complete, it doesn't speed things up. It doesn't really have a particular tempo at all, and greater efficiency doesn't make it run faster—it just goes along.

The bubbling up of events in the field of time is not an alarming, external thing, as it was in the early Stages. It's just a little tickle, enlivening our play as each bubble pops open and a new situation is revealed. We become free in all this, but not necessarily efficient. Our real expertise is in *relaxing* into things as they are, without any narrow notions of control. So we're not burdened by technical efficiency or by the expectations that come from thinking of ourselves as experts.

At times the Earthly Hsien seems master of circumstances, and at other times he's mastered by circumstances. It's a play or dance where he is definitely hooked up to EIGHT and NINE, but he's not overly concerned about knowing or controlling every detail of what's happening. He's not necessarily "brilliant" or "meticulous."

So the Immortal is completely at play and often a bit stream-tossed, according to the current, and yet at times it's very easy for him to stand against circumstances and do whatever he pleases. He may even play at being an obstruction for a while—that is also one of the possibilities his free action explores and expresses. After all, Nature is not a machine trundling along inexorably in a particular direction.

The point is not that his control is erratic or that he's very powerful some of the time, but that mastery in terms of control *isn't the issue* and he's big enough to include both mastery and being mastered, just as his life includes life and death. The Way is not just the accumulation of energy or being powerful all the time.

The play of all dichotomies and the cycles of Yin and Yang and the Elements are being very clearly demonstrated by his actions, but are also being demonstrated *to* him as well. They're saturating his entire life.

The impact of such matters is felt when we act them out. While SEVEN, EIGHT, and NINE are really beyond the activities of a mortal or an immortal *being,* at TEN they all get acted out, simultaneously revealed and demonstrated, back and forth, by and to the Earthly Hsien. Again, the Image reflects this atmosphere of play. He strikes a dancing pose, dancing and being danced around by Nature.

So, what is already the same about the individual shen and the Tao itself now demonstrates itself in all our actions. Anything we *or the world* does at TEN is motivated by the natural polarity of union, and this is the real idea in saying that "everything in daily life is yoga." The Hsien's dance shows this both to himself and to others.

> *The movements of his dance are spontaneous but highly instructive to all beings who encounter him.*

This dance reflects his participation in the Way, and also teaches and facilitates it for others. To paraphrase one of my teachers:

> "We exist within a world of ordinary events. In this world we are an accumulation of events without illumination. Intersecting this world of ordinary events are many extraordinary luminous worlds such as the realm of the Hsien. Earthly Hsien recognize and demonstrate the skills of living in both ordinary and extraordinary worlds simultaneously. But those people who do not practice cultivation and are confused, collect events as personal property, declaring the 'self' to be real and true. They suffer deeply and must live as soldiers in a long losing battle.

The Hsien inhales the extraordinary and exhales the world of events. His subtle activities, for those who can 'see,' demonstrate a direct path to the immortal realms. To use extraordinary means in the event world is not better but is merely used to get our attention. Hsien who choose to live on mountains, far from others, work still nearer the Source of event worlds. They too demonstrate the Way, but on subtler levels."

The Earthly Hsien dances spontaneously to the rhythms of EIGHT and the steps of NINE, demonstrating both in SEVEN's Space of freedom. His movements alternately mirror, avoid, and deflect the lines of power running through the multi-dimensional environment (the same lines that form the basis of feng shui—geomancy).

Instructive and helpful, the Hsien inspires and protects others without manipulation. He uses his insight to express his own personal affinities and his gratitude toward other beings. He may do this in a very ordinary or a very extraordinary manner, choosing the type of time in which he wishes to operate, based on the occasion and needs of those with whom he interacts.

Someone who is caught up in the Hsien's action might well report a story like "I met this fellow along the road. We had some wine and chatted, and later he invited me to join him for dinner at home. So we had a fantastic meal, and drank all night. In the morning, I found myself back by the side of the road, and 40 years had passed here ... but I have not aged."

Such stories abound in Chinese literature, and the possibilities they suggest often frighten the practical, family-oriented Chinese, making them want to avoid the Immortal's activity and habitat ... but the story could also go other ways. The Earthly Hsien might instruct someone for 40 years and then give him some gold and put him back in his original time. In either case, when the story is finally told, it will be clear that the Hsien drank with this person and was in his world, but showed that world itself to be enfolded within another and larger type of time and space, demonstrating the interplay of ordinariness and extraordinariness.

161

TYING UP LOOSE ENDS

At EIGHT, it became clear that cultivation is largely a process of completing our ordinary approach to activities. Empowered by EIGHT and NINE, the Earthly Hsien's actions naturally conclude entanglements and tie up loose ends. Some of these were caused by the desires, beliefs, and habits of Monkey, Sage, and Mountain, but many others derive from our attempts to fix these at FIVE.

People at FIVE tend to believe they must cope with problems accumulated from ONE through FOUR. But since the view of cultivation at FIVE is rather small and obsessive, tinkering around with yogic manipulations of chi and attention there may leave residual kinks.

The Earthly Hsien addresses these odds and ends, but without effort or any sense of burden or concern for improvement. He's not duty bound to fix things, and doesn't feel that he himself has old karma to eliminate. Rather, his action is like a respiratory process going back and forth among the Stages, putting things in their proper perspective of SEVEN, EIGHT, and NINE. These latter stages are essentially natural respiratory poles for the entire Way.

This is the respiration of the universe, rather than of a human being climbing some sort of ladder. We're not leaving things behind as we go on, we're just breathing more fully, back to all the early stages and forward all the way to TWELVE.

> He simply eats when hungry, sleeps when tired, and plays when inspired, yet the profundity of such activity reverberates like thunder over the Earth.

The Earthly Hsien is very comfortable dancing in the midst of all that's ordinary and familiar. The world is his place of 'sorcery,' and he sees that was really always the case. So he experiences no surprise upon finding himself back at the mountain peak with a human form. And his actions do not alternate between SEVEN's spontaneity and EIGHT's precision, but simply show that Order is spontaneous and that ordinary humanness operates in an enormous field of freedom.

This integrated quality continuously ignites and enriches itself, drawing on the strength of basic actions that are appropriate to our nature and situation. The Hsien relies on no external guide or rule, but has relaxed into the full potency of NINE's finding the real (but still ordinary) world manifesting through EIGHT's Order and SEVEN's freedom.

Each of the Hsien's actions has a definite front and back. He acts in whatever ordinary way is necessary to carry on with his life, but each action is so open in scope and interconnected with Nature that it may also unify dualities and resolve conflicts in many different spheres.

To take a very mundane example, he may be thirsty, drink a cup of tea, and thereby facilitate a fundamental shift or balance in Nature. He might serve tea to a grumpy friend and thereby harmonize all that has ever occurred between them and also between everyone like the friend and all of those with the need to give. Even when he's alone or interacting with only a few people, the Hsien's gestures are universally significant.

His simple actions, like eating when hungry, "reverberate like thunder over the earth," because he is a conduit through which the forces of Nature are being funnelled and expressed, and each action is as natural as a thunderstorm or a moonbeam.

If at TEN the cultivator is grateful for his food or takes care of his own respiratory system, that sets up a momentum throughout the universe. This is one reason why Taoists emphasize diet and hygiene practices, and don't necessarily say much about compassion. Their actions are their expression of humility and generosity ... they act 'locally' with the global result that the respiratory and digestive systems of Nature function without obstruction. The satisfaction and harmony of such systems contributes much to the general order of things.

This scope of action makes TEN a place of tremendous joy, beyond any thought of accomplishing a worthy purpose but deriving from being completely in a dance operating on many levels. Everything within the Hsien's sphere of influence participates in this joy and self-liberating action. He's not merely enjoying the resolution of 'problems' ... he's resolving even the fundamental dualisms in phenomena, the endless facets of polarity reflected in his dance. So Yin and Yang are becoming more complimentary with every simple gesture.

At TEN we feel the 'tension' of polarity as an amusing tickle which just becomes a little more intense as we bring the polar qualities together ... there's a fluttering or slightly nervous character to our unifying action, but in union itself the ticklish tension is released into joy. It's very similar to the initial sensation of chi moving through our channels in yogic practice—after things get running, the special sensation evaporates and we return to the more broadly-based ordinariness of human experience.

This unifying action and 'sealing' sensation constitute the recurring themes of the Hsien's life at TEN, and involve no moments or movements that interrupt his dance. So, on various intersecting levels, the Hsien is playfully sorting things out, clearing the way for letting everything operate as part of a Return to the Source, the completion of the Way.

TEN

SECTION III: THE DANCE OF COMPLETION

As was true in the previous Stages, the cultivator is still involved in an erotic courtship between Chaos and Order, expressed through his dance. But at TEN, he's moving in the light, taking Order's side. And he flirts, teases and "dances things about" to unmask and undress them rather than to clothe and ornament them.

The Hsien's action exposes the familiar world's more subtle principles and the alluring, mysterious darkness of Chaos underlying them. TEN's fully mature Third Eye then appreciates the familiar and the primordial Origin as a unity.

The Hsien's fluid dance sustains a light, principle-oriented ordinariness, with no residue of intent. Slipping into ELEVEN can thus happen spontaneously.

The Earthly Hsien's activity and the Way itself are riddled with paradoxes. Just at the point where he's regained his body and found the possibility of making it totally viable, even immortal, and also found the complete role of his individuality in the world, the Hsien releases it all again.

The Hsien acts to open up and free life to fulfill itself. But this means both to enjoy life fully as it is and also to let it go on. Life then completes itself by participating in the great transformative processes underlying transmogrification in ELEVEN and TWELVE (fundamental change to reveal what is always true).

The Earthly Hsien's dance exercises the NINE facet of his presence, emphasizing our unity with the earth, sun, moon, mountains, rivers, etc.—we *are* manifest Nature. His dance also lightly opens beyond the details of our self image, including and celebrating EIGHT. This shows that what's really familiar about our form and individuality is not our particular face, features, coloring, height, and mannerisms, but the matters of basic principle—Yin and Yang and the Elements in Order. Taken together, these insights of NINE and EIGHT support our existence as the Heavenly Hsien at ELEVEN, where we live with the manifest physical universe itself as our body.

The Earthly Hsien's dance further flows with the world of Order into Chaos, thus highlighting the nonduality in Order and Chaos. This presages the movement to TWELVE and the dragon's nesting in the darkness of SEVEN's Space while also flying freely through the Gate of Duality into the Source.

In anticipating both ELEVEN and TWELVE in his dances, the Earthly Hsien is not causing anything. He's paving an extremely subtle Way here, based in SEVEN, which is quite different from our usual cause-effect thinking and does not involve leaps to new heights or lead away from our current situation.

Spiritual paths that lead to a peak experience all ended at SIX ... goals, peak experiences, and the common, gross notion of 'experience' in general are not the issue anymore. The Way completely obviates that old approach.

The Earthly Hsien's dance in the territory of SEVEN through TEN doesn't reject life in any way, but actually keeps us in it. And being really in it naturally leads to its completion, possibly involving death as an appropriate preliminary.

DEATH AND COMPLETION

The transition to ELEVEN may or may not include physical death. But it is at least the completion of an approach to individual physical existence which characterizes all the Stages through TEN.

This is also why the *artfulness* of the Hsien is depicted in TEN's Image. It's an art that dances us away from an existence based on conditions and sings a song of impending completion—not entirely a happy theme—yet the artful singing of it elevates it to a sort of joy. The sensitivity and balance of the artist are also required to vigorously demonstrate our experience in the world and to simultaneously complete it, so that nothing is left unfinished.

If death does occur at TEN, it's still likely that everything required to clear the way for ELEVEN and TWELVE will have been done. And we also know that nothing 'real'—as we came to understand that term in SEVEN—actually dies here. The experience of going from FIVE to SEVEN was actually more of a death than is the experience of physical death at TEN or later. Here it's not really seen as an end, but as a very satisfying experience. So if death is looming at TEN, the conditions that would make it anything but a satisfying experience are those which need to be ironed out.

The artistry and thoroughness of which the Hsien is capable usually assure that everything needful is handled. If that isn't possible, then the cultivator will arrange a long pause in some other 'state,' permitting a resolution and eventual return to the main issues of the Way.

Perhaps the simplest example of a condition that must be satisfied at TEN is that we retain enough chi to make the transition to ELEVEN. If physical death is part of our experience of TEN, then the Earthly Hsien dances and balances the factors of his life so that death does not come before continuation of the Way is secured.

In particular, the Hsien participates without fear in the cycles of both accumulation and loss of chi—the respiration of energy—that are a natural part of life, but he avoids losing any energy needlessly. He sees what is appropriate and does not spend energy on ambition or aggression of any sort.

This view is reflected in even the early Stages, which is why aggression is contraindicated for Monkey and Sage. However, while Monkey and Sage may forswear aggression, they still spend energy ... it's the only way they know to approach life. The Hsien is focussed on life as a process of discovery, has no enemies, and cultivates the Way without any spending. His action is truly respiratory, recharging by nature, and this is the basis of his 'immortality.'

So, in various ways, TEN is looking back to SEVEN and ahead to ELEVEN and TWELVE, perhaps considering death but not seeing it as something to seek or avoid at all costs. If some fatal disease arises at TEN, it's accepted and understood to be ELEVEN and TWELVE arising. The face of transformation and unity might indeed be disease and death. The Hsien doesn't have to achieve anything except opening himself to a larger field of existence, and that's not thwarted by life processes and phases.

Above all, TEN is a Stage of *activity,* and the last activity possible (in the sense of a 'doing') along the Way is the fertilization of our understanding to expand beyond all restrictive notions of individuality and of individual, specific physicality as necessities of existence. This final act of the Earthly Hsien 'fathers' a totally new vision of life as Being at ELEVEN.

ELEVEN is a pose of life that is minimally reactive, high-lighting the feeling of merging effortlessly with Nature and living through all Its processes.

ELEVEN

SECTION I: THE HEAVENLY HSIEN

At ELEVEN the Heavenly Hsien brings forth the infinite possibilities of Being in the form of an egg seated in the first Heavenly Chamber of his body.

ELEVEN is already the completion of the Way. It's not a prelude to something higher, but one aspect of the Way's fruition. Specifically, it's the cultivator's demonstration of the action of manifest Nature, the knowable Tao.

OPENING TO THE HEAVENLY HSIEN

The Earthly Hsien danced out the last residual conditions of human-ness in the space of SEVEN, EIGHT, and NINE, enabling him to appreciate human life fully. So he sees his action and that of the universe (NINE), and natural laws (EIGHT) and fundamental open-ness (SEVEN) as all being basically the same. This frees up all notions of activity in the familiar earthly sense, opening the way to the existence of the Heavenly Hsien, shown in ELEVEN's Image in an 'immovable' meditation posture.

The Heavenly Hsien does not 'act' or 'move' in the old way. He's engaged in a process of gestation. Within the center of his body there's an egg, the "egg before everything." As his last gesture, the Heavenly

Hsien is bringing forth the "Tao from within" so it may meet the "outer Tao" (manifest Nature).

The egg is the potential to be anything or everything that can occur, including ONE through TEN. The Heavenly Hsien doesn't transcend humanness in order to act on a more universal level. Rather, in an extraordinary expression of self respect and compassion, he gathers everything we appeared to be in the time of the earlier Stages, and incubates it in the egg to bring out the full import of what was really involved. This is a process of complete recapitulation and rejuvenation of humanness.

All the experiences we've discussed have been retained, not left behind at TEN. Now they're seen together and at once, as constituting one unified, quite perfect, aspect of the Way. But they're also seen as representing just a tiny part of the egg's potential, since the whole human experience fills only a miniscule portion of the egg. With this understanding, the Fourth Eye's appreciation of our nature and full place in Nature become completely mature.

Since ONE through TEN are present in the Heavenly Hsien at ELEVEN, they actually participate in the ultimate and impending Return to the Source. But they have assumed a proper perspective which doesn't obscure the larger movements of Nature. All are nurtured and expressed, while also being taken back to their primordial context of Originating Source.

The Earthly Hsien's activity was essentially a way of fertilizing the egg of the Heavenly Hsien, who then, being pregnant, is still and inward-dwelling. This fertilization process at TEN was the last 'doing' that can occur. The Heavenly Hsien doesn't do anything, but IS. The Earthly Hsien's activity concluded or resolved all of its conditions, so a new view of existence, of Being, may then express itself.

It's important to note that the fertilizing activity of TEN does not *cause* ELEVEN. Neither ELEVEN nor TWELVE have any causal antecedents. The Heavenly Hsien's entire being is saturated by "no cause" … no one deserves or achieves ELEVEN. The real scale and nature of the living universe's activity are now revealed, but it's impossible to say, in ordinary causal terms, how this happened.

The Earthly Hsien played freely in an enormous field, but the Heavenly Hsien's Being is beyond even those notions of enormity … so he doesn't play, he has no residues of causes and conditions to define an agenda. ELEVEN and TWELVE are two faces of the same truth, with ELEVEN being the more Yin image, rigid in being pregnant with potential, while TWELVE is the more Yang image, the pure quality of unrestrained movement (which also doesn't act in the ordinary, small time-bound sense).

Both ELEVEN and TWELVE are beyond duality. They represent the last two images that those of us left in duality can have—the Yin egg and the Yang dragon.

Like the yogi at NINE, the Heavenly Hsien is living in the very center of creative energy. But unlike the former, who must experiment with this energy and practice acting as Source, the Heavenly Hsien demonstrates complete mastery of originating energy without having to do or try anything. At ELEVEN, there's no on-off quality to our being at Source … it's continuous and nondualistic.

The seemingly ordinary activity of TEN has refined (the Heavenly Hsien's) Earthly form into the pure components of Nature, allowing him to manifest any or all things under Heaven.

The cultivator may experience a physical death at TEN before emerging as the Heavenly Hsien, but that's not a prerequisite of any sort. Whether he died at TEN or is still sitting on his cushion, at ELEVEN he has a very different type of physicality, characteristic of the Heavenly Hsien and permitting both gestation of the egg and a new type of 'action.' Such new possibilities arise at ELEVEN because the Heavenly Hsien's body has become subtlety itself, entirely a thing of the energy realm.

At ELEVEN, energy is experienced most clearly and broadly as what we and Nature are. The body and energy are both transformed here to represent the Heavenly Hsien, but life is not the product of a relationship between two things anymore. The emphasis is more on energy per se than on the forms and apparent material 'stuff' associated with energy's more complex and stratified patterns.

173

The Heavenly Hsien's 'body' is thoroughly constituted by Nature's principles. So, all physicalness becomes available to the Cultivator at ELEVEN (rather than one specific kind of physicalness).

Since the Heavenly Hsien is exposed by TEN's dancing individuality into the living universe of NINE and the principles of EIGHT, the Heavenly Hsien manifests like the subtle tides and currents of power acting on the world. Whereas the Earthly Hsien demonstrated his existence by individuating himself from these tidal energies, the Heavenly Hsien lives through and as them all.

The Earthly Hsien stood out among these natural forms and tides, but was still characterized by those on which he rode into TEN. He arose the way all phenomena do, so there's no special system that he used to exist, act, or survive death. Whether he died at TEN or not, he remained essentially part of the energy currents moving through the universe. The Heavenly Hsien is simply the most complete expression of such an existence, totally comfortable operating that way without any reservations or limits.

We can say that some sort of individuality survives in ELEVEN, but that it does so without any nervousness about its survival or about preserving its discreteness and unique integrity. It trusts the Great Order of Nature to manage the book-keeping of "personal identity," and swims freely in and as all the forms and currents of Nature. This is possible only when the experience of living is largely an energetic one, rather than one linked to a particular bodily form.

"HIS EYES BECAME SUN AND MOON"

The Heavenly Hsien could become a drop in the Pacific ocean, swept by gargantuan tides, seemingly lost, and yet jump out again and go right into the eye of a sailor. Thus, as a tear, he could reintegrate with a particular human life. The possibilities are infinitely diverse.

So the Heavenly Hsien could be the 'king' of many world systems, but could also become a tear drop. This is feasible because life's energy component could be as broadly-based as light and maintain individuality, and the body could be as general as an "organic soup" and not be lost, regardless of the forms it takes. For example, such a 'soup' might be organized into something as specific as a mosquito. If someone swatted the mosquito and thereby sent that 'body' back into a nondescript state of moisture in thousands of different worlds, this would still not disturb the Heavenly Hsien at all.

Ordinarily, we are quite easily tumbled into paranoid preoccupations with particular physical characteristics and with the safety of our physical form. But the Heavenly Hsien enjoys a very complete sense of freedom and trust in Nature. The entire path that began at ONE and has now opened to ELEVEN is characterized by a growing trust in the human relationship to Nature. The transition from SIX to SEVEN reaffirmed that trust, and ELEVEN seals it forever.

This is not a trust that emerges through a deal, a breakthrough experience or revelation. It's nurtured at every point of the Way, steadily growing until it's possible to have a body as great as all the seas in all the worlds without being nervous about it. There's no basis for a reaction like "it's getting too big, I can't keep it together!" My teacher from Hebei once said to me: "you could become a monkey's fart ... it doesn't matter, and you really can't hold on anymore."

The Heavenly Hsien could become the mist hovering between remote mountain peaks, or a distant star exhibiting generosity by actually feeding the physicality and energy of beings through its light. Similarly, he may simultaneously assume a variety of physical expressions in different times. The whole notion of embodiment has now broken out of the limitations of Sage and Monkey, been recast by the instruction of EIGHT and NINE, and has moved beyond even that instruction.

The shen, summary experience of humanness has united with the entire space of Nature, and so is quite comfortable seeing its functioning body and energy in a universal way. Thus at ELEVEN, we accept that we really *are* Nature's manifesting principle in its phase of physicalness. Recognizing that our energy pattern 'skeleton' is EIGHT, our physical form and environment are NINE, and our activity is the dance of TEN, we experience living concretely at ELEVEN without any waiting.

175

The personal environment of the Heavenly Hsien is not some rarified space inhabited only by a special person. As we've said, it's the most enormous possible sense of personal space, now coequal with the space of Nature Itself, so it also constitutes the context of all human beings. It therefore has an influence on all of us … the Heavenly Hsien is already living through us, and we participate in his perspective and sense of connection with Nature.

SHARING THE WAY BUT LEAVING NO MARKS

We live inside the sphere of the Heavenly Hsien, and he in turn may enter our existence in various ways to facilitate our own cultivation. This is considered possible because the Heavenly Hsien is so close to the Source—which really vivifies everything from moment to moment—that he can enter a particular being's life without experiencing any obstruction and without disturbing that being in any way. He might become a pig one day, and teach compassion to a farmer by his actions as a pig.

One of the most important differences between TEN and ELEVEN is that the quality of action changes at ELEVEN, and this is another reason why the Heavenly Hsien can share our existence in a thoroughly unobtrusive way. If he instructs us, it feels like ordinary inspiration, not 'possession' or intervention. If he acts through us, it's an action founded in the same principles that we express anyway and not a radical departure. More generally, his influence isn't really "on and off" like ordinary action … it's quite universalized, continuous, and thus goes beyond what people can ordinarily notice. The Heavenly Hsien's whole sense of existence and activity is so *quintessentially* what we really are that it doesn't make any overt impression on us.

This change in the character of the cultivator's action began at EIGHT, where events and actions were seen to be expressions of a Great Order which is quite invisible to people in the earlier Stages. But the Heavenly Hsien's very existence or mode of being represents such a fully realized relationship with Nature, and responds to a such a huge context, he virtually disappears from the human view.

He doesn't really "leave earth and go to heaven"—he just enters into the essence of natural process and humanness without going anywhere at all. This is true even if he's a cultivator who did not experience death at TEN and continues to express himself in our world through his original human body.

Since the polarity of dualism is extinguished at ELEVEN, there's no need for the Heavenly Hsien in human form to concern himself with it or with worldly circumstance. There's no agenda or movement or interaction with others in the ordinary way. The popular image of the Heavenly Hsien is thus of someone who lives quite remote from the world, or has left the world altogether. For this reason, the Image shows him in a 'retreat' setting. But again, this doesn't mean the Hsien has rejected the world or is hiding from it ... he has simply taken it in its fullness and resides in its heart.

If we don't act in ways related to the web of typical causes and conditions, then physical movement changes, physicalness itself becomes subtle, and our 'tracks' are quickly lost. So it's very likely that few people will know us or have our complete personal history. Sometimes traditions say that such cultivators manifest and act heroically out of compassion for sentient beings. But really it's just a "going on" and there's no way to describe the 'why' of it at all in ordinary terms.

This trackless quality is also cultivated in the stages leading up to ELEVEN. Taoists often revere cultivators of the past, about whom nothing is known except that their cultivation escaped all notice, because this is a version of "being outside of all conditions." For the Heavenly Hsien, this form of discretion is a natural consequence of his nature, but for those at SEVEN through TEN it's a sign of great skill.

For example, in the past some cultivators took on roles that allowed people to discard them, to pigeon-hole them as being beneath notice, so that they could slide through conditions. They became pork butchers, or even monks with slightly 'improper' behavior, causing them to lose the consideration of their community.

Such a concern for discretion in cultivation is very important at every stage. People often strive to do extraordinary and magical things, as though that were the measure of the Way. But my teachers felt that one should not go to extremes—"don't be a general or a saint."

It's better for a cultivator to appear very plain—that's what cultivation is anyway. If someone should want to make a demonstration of the Way for others, he could wait until life's end. He might then die in an extraordinary manner that shows the full scope of the human relationship to Nature, but doesn't reinforce typical notions like 'virtue' or 'heroism' (or other forms of specialness founded in the views of Monkey and Sage).

The fruit of cultivation shouldn't be reduced to a skill or rearrangement of our characteristics and causal conditions. Cultivation is about looking into what we are, pealing conditions away by putting them in their real context, and then demonstrating that context—not some personal skill or moral virtue—to others. And if it really does become necessary to exercise strength or skill in a situation, it might be better to use those associated with avoidance rather than with aggression.

The ultimate dream of most religions is to establish a supremely powerful worldly king. It's a popular fantasy to imagine that someone will transcend the world and then turn around to rule it, and people are always building thrones for such rulers. But nobody who has come to live in the context of the Heavenly Hsien would ever sit on such a throne. Only someone who made a quick foray into SEVEN and then returned to SIX would accept the job.

In any case, this desire for a ruler from heaven is usually frustrated, and so people pretend that it's happening or that it happened in some "golden age" of the past. But in fact it never happens in ordinary historical time, only in the time of the Heavenly Hsien.

The Hsien doesn't need enthronement. 'He'—the energy in which he participates—is the ruler of the world anyway, or at least carries some aspects of that function, without adulation or a special seat. His is an invisible reign, and while his purpose may include the ordinary world and its affairs, it also has a far greater scope, founded deep within his Being. As master of the Fourth Eye, he commingles with all livingness, human and nonhuman, on every scale.

ELEVEN

SECTION II: THE DRAGON'S EGG

At the very center of the rather universalized 'body' of the Heavenly Hsien, the essence of his life processes naturally work to complete the cultivation of all human possibilities in the perspective of the Tao. The Image of ELEVEN shows this process as the nourishing of an egg containing these possibilities in their real medium or context.

When the egg opens, the Dragon of TWELVE—embodying all that the egg contains—flies free, physically manifesting nonduality and nondual action in every sphere. The appearance of the Dragon is the transition from ELEVEN to TWELVE. Here we will limit our discussion to the 'hatching' of the egg in ELEVEN.

If the cultivator at ELEVEN is using a human body to 'bear' the egg, there sometimes are very marked signs of the egg's maturation, which may result in or accompany the death of the body. For example, there may be very dramatic visual displays or changes in the surrounding atmospheric temperature, or remarkable scents or sounds.

To my own grief, regret, and joy, this happened with one of my own masters. My teacher from Hebei province had established himself for the last several decades in a hermitage in the mountains of Northern Taiwan. Late in 1978, he called me for a chat, and essentially explained that he was "going away." I didn't realize until later what he really meant, but in any case, we discussed issues related to my being more

179

on my own in the future. He emphasized that confidence and the correct transmission of the lineage derived from remaining true to one's own experience.

Essentially, he was recommending that I trust myself, that even uncertainty or confusion are valid and useful because they are simply ONE through SIX, which have their truth and their place in the Way. He said that, just as it sometimes seems in those early Stages, the Way really cannot be 'accomplished.' It can't be accomplished but it also doesn't need to be—real cultivation is not that sort of activity! He had made the same point on many previous occasions, but this time he communicated it with such force and clarity that it crystallized and finalized my own understanding.

Discussing the issue of his departure in the broadest possible sense, he explained that it was called a Return because the unknowableness of where he was going matched that of where we had all come from. People generally think that, in order to act confidently, you must know where you're going and where you're "coming from." But my teacher was claiming that in fact, confidence derives from decisively acknowledging the unknowable aspect of the Tao, experiencing and drawing strength from its unfathomably vast potency, rather than from diminishing ourselves and It by pinning it down.

After our talk, he returned to his retreat. About a month later, he demonstrated what, since the early Han dynasty, Taoists have traditionally called "liberation from the corpse."

Over a period of several days, sitting in a fixed posture, he broadcast beams of 'light' through the gaps in the walls of his hermitage and across the entire valley. This demonstration was concluded by a cracking sound that appeared to originate right next to each person in the valley. Such a sound is traditionally considered an aspect of the death of Taoists in remote areas, signalling to cultivators on other mountains that one of their fellows is departing.

This master's hermitage was finally opened on the tenth day after these signs began. His body had disappeared, leaving only clothes on his cushion, long bear claw-like nails, and hair. The clothes had become saturated by a reddish powdery substance exuded by his final physical processes, and were thus sufficiently stiffened to remain in an upright 'sitting' posture. My friend and teacher had departed forever, but in a way that placed him at the heart of my own life and inspiration.

THE BODY OF LIGHT

As my late teacher demonstrated, the phenomenon of the "body of light" is very real. In fact, various versions of it are discussed in many different meditation and shamanic traditions.

Among the many images people have contrived for the Tao, one of the most common is pure light. The Cultivator of the Way who demonstrates the Body of Light is decisively acknowledging the Tao, making a Return which really lacks movement but is a very definite, direct discernment of the Source *as such*. Different systems of practice facilitate this discernment and acknowledgment in different ways, but the main point is always total clarity about our nature as being the Tao.

If we were pressed to explain this Return as an *action,* we might then say the Cultivator sees that the body and energy have comprised his being, and that once *released,* they 'leave' only their Originating Source. Releasing to the Tao 'rips' the composed bubble of personal existence and lets the Tao shine through. This reveals our original or true face.

The Tao's 'light' isn't one which could be vanquished or obscured, nor is it more or less bright than any other form of light. It's just the 'original light,' not really a visual phenomenon at all, because it's not something that could be looked at, dualistically, by a separate perceiver. When people are in the proximity of the demonstration of the Body of Light, they essentially 'imagine' and project light onto a profound energy experience which really cannot be apprehended in any ordinary way. Such displays are much more than special effects—they clarify the relationship of human desires, perceptions, and memories to Originating Source.

181

Preparation for the Body of Light may begin years before the cultivator's death. Traditional hygiene and yogic practices are used during life, both to accumulate this energy and to distill or refine it, turning quantity into quality. Such refinement is important, since retaining too much of the energy associated with ordinary robustness produces a kind of physicality that's difficult to release at death.

A cultivator nearing the end of life may seem rather frail, but may in fact be turning 'crystalline.' Traditionally, Taoist yogis preparing for death spend part of their final retreat by stopping the production of the common "worker bee" energy altogether, isolating what remains, and then explicitly shedding or exuding it. For, this energy is a facet of the Tao which naturally moves into manifestation and in that sense would resist going back to the Source. So it is best released into the human realm, which can still benefit from it. Cultivating it during life and then shedding it decisively at death keeps such energy where it belongs.

Such a forceful, 'yogic' shedding of energy contributes to the visual flaring and other manifestations which observers note during the demonstration of the Body of Light. It's important to note, by the way, that this energy is shed firmly but without any *rejection*.

Of course, like many Taoists of the past, we modern cultivators might approach death in a less forceful and technical manner, focussing precisely on the Tao and allowing what should be shed to gradually separate itself off and dissipate. This still makes the right point, and is quite different from the typical "death by exhaustion" or bodily failure which lacks the power and discernment to make a "clean break," and thus also lacks the appreciation of Returning to the Source.

DEMONSTRATIONS OF DEATH

This is a basic description of a cultivator's transmogrification at ELEVEN (generally, but not always, a death). One of the most important things about a death at ELEVEN is that, however remarkable it may seem, it is still a characteristically human death, distinguished from the deaths of most people only in its definiteness ... it's simply a *very* "clean break," and proclaims the enormity of the human situation.

Usually, people are less aware of what their lives consist of, and so die in a way that also returns to the Source, but with far less incisiveness. Their components, form and energy, remain somewhat mixed for a time after death, leaving a corpse that undergoes slower transformative processes. The import of death, of Return, thus remains somewhat muddled. Of course, both approaches to death 'count,' simply because both happen.

Someone who dies understanding Return clearly reveals the 'light' of the Tao in which all observers, all human beings, actually participate. Conversely, someone who dies by exhaustion communicates a different message to others on the energy level—such a death is experienced by observers as a subtle dark 'implosion' or in a feeling that something has been taken out of them. It's like a light going out, a loss, rather than a light shooting off to reveal an even greater underlying luminosity.

However, an ordinary person who has not cultivated the full vigor of the Way may nevertheless die smiling and with a deep sense of lightness and completion ... this is often and quite rightly called "dying in grace." This too expresses the luminous quality of the energy body and is another, more familiar way to demonstrate the Body of Light.

Like Chuang Tzu in the distant past, cultivators who are rather philosophically inclined or emphasize pure contemplation methods would laugh at someone employing yogic technique to 'achieve' the Body of Light. But in that very critique, they might demonstrate their own readiness for a profound death without requiring any specific methodology.

We needn't see such a criticism as a true rejection of yoga but rather as an injunction to remember the key point—the human relationship to Nature, as it is, without unnatural additions. By poking fun at advanced yogic demonstrations, some Taoist philosophers help keep these extraordinary gestures in proper perspective, showing the 'right' way to understand them and, perhaps, to perform them or even decline them.

The Body of Light is simply one example of the outcome of consciously staying in the core of natural process, without aggressive desires or struggle. It's a perfectly natural and human gesture, and is moved into a supernatural category only by the perception of observers, not by that of the cultivator himself, who participates joyously in the full scope of both his life and his death. The point is not to preserve the body against decay but to include it in the experience of death, so that everything may then find its true place.

SLEEP AND DEATH

As various traditions have pointed out, the process of death is like that of falling asleep in some ways. Both are opportunities to unfold and experience the complete landscape of our nature and Nature Itself by releasing the pressing issues and restrictions of daily life.

Normally, people approach sleep in an exhausted and heedless state, with the result that they fall through much of the landscape of experience available there ... by the time they regain awareness, it's as an entry into various dreams that correspond to the usual logic of their lives. Much more is actually available in sleep, and by missing it, we fail to experience ourselves within a full perspective. We therefore essentially trap certain dimensions of our humanness inside us, creating an incentive to "try again" the next day so they may surface.

In the full experience of a human death, we may find and acknowledge all the Stages we've discussed, and retain the freedom to wander in them until we have a mature understanding of their connection to the Source. If we fall heedlessly through these experiences due to a limited or exhausted participation in death—so that SEVEN through TWELVE are not visited and seen as part of what we are—we trap the Tao inside of our energy. New births and lives are then naturally instigated to express the Tao, to "bring it out."

THE EMERGENCE OF THE DRAGON

A complete participation in our universalized life at ELEVEN and also, perhaps, in our very human but thoroughly-explored death, results in our hatching the Dragon's egg. To review, nurturing that egg involved gathering all the facets of humanness back to the center of our Being, letting them gestate there so that we could give birth to the fullness of all that we are.

We then brought forth everything in its most potentiated and extended form. We also let each aspect go to its proper place within Nature and complete itself. We thereby came to understand Being as including birth and death rather than beginning at birth and ending at death.

Our nature now emerges in its full freedom, no longer differentiable from the widest and most profoundly central aspects of Nature. As its last action in ELEVEN, it makes a motionless Return to the Source by backing into its true nature (i.e., 'going' to where it really always was) as the Dragon of TWELVE.

TWELVE's Dragon simultaneously embodies *all* types of human experience, since what these share is the very heart, not the 'goal,' of life.

TWELVE

SECTION I: RETURN TO THE SOURCE

At TWELVE the Gate of Yin and Yang again appears, beyond which lies the Originating Source itself, represented by the open circle. Above the circle, the Dragon—born from the egg at ELEVEN—flies in every possible space, thus representing the Freedom of Primordial Energy.

Our Dragon nature now fearlessly declares itself, roaring and cavorting, not as the culmination of the Way but as its essence. ELEVEN doesn't really lead to TWELVE ... they are two co-equal facets of Being. The complement to the rigid posture and indwelling potency of ELEVEN is thus revealed in the unrestrained flight of the Dragon. The Gate of Duality, symbolic of all the realms of phenomena, is now placed in a nonproblematical relationship with the Originating Source, and the Dragon flies without any concern about limiting boundaries.

THE DRAGON

At ELEVEN and TWELVE, the full character of the Way's inclusiveness has emerged. Even apparently incompatible things are simultaneously accommodated ... thus, we could tell the story of the Dragon in different ways.

187

Focussing on the Dragon's form, we could say that the Dragon is the fully-forged, truly *integral* form of the cultivator, consisting of neither body nor energy nor any other 'component' as these were previously seen. The Dragon form is the true nature of our supposed 'components' in ONE through ELEVEN, and encompasses all possible forms at once.

At TWELVE individual components like the body and energy have become as characterless as the shen, and the difference between them and the infinitely-faceted Tao itself dissolves in union. So the cultivator is distinctly embodied here as an individuality which is neither composed nor limited, and has both no characteristics and all characteristics whatsoever.

This Dragon is all muscle and enormously heavy and yet can fly, has stubby legs and yet runs faster than any horse. It's both creative and destructive, holds pure Yin in one hand and pure Yang in the other, and yet is neither.

The Dragon encompasses all dualities and composed or characterized things and yet, just like the egg it arises from at ELEVEN, is far more than the sum of them all. It is the nondual existence forged from all dualities, a forging that took place before, during, and after the journey through the 'territory' in which we seem to be composed creatures. It cannot ever be *achieved* by any effort and doesn't need to be.

Regarding the Dragon's action, we could say simply that the Dragon represents freedom. Or we could follow traditional mythology and say that the Dragon is important as the last stage of cultivation because only he is sufficiently powerful to fly all the way to 'heaven.' That is, only the Dragon can reach the Gate of Duality and succeed in passing on to the Originating Source. Actually, that's where he is, in one sense, so "getting there" is no problem at all. He is 'there' without being at any distance from the other Stages. So he can fly right back through the Gate and reenter phenomena.

We could even say that passing through the Gate to the Source and coming back to phenomena is a dynamic feature saturating every instant of every Stage, every breath. This unimpeded access is fundamental to the Dragon's nature. The Dragon's bi-directional flight is a gesture performed without any motive other than freedom. It's the *primordial* gesture of the Tao itself, an unfathomably free wriggling motion stretching in the directions of both the Source and all the Stages.

This energetic wriggling 'does' nothing at all. And yet, it is the very fabric of all livingness, all Time.

Lord of the worlds, all governed by EIGHT's principles, but nesting in his dark unknowable lair at SEVEN, the Dragon is all paradox. This just means he assumes the one image of our relationship to Nature that's sufficiently multi-dimensional to be *true.*

He's still familiar on the level of *principle,* but the actual details of his form are strange to us. His form is new, unfamiliar—it's specifically that form which is free within principle, not compelled to follow the dualistic phases of all other physical forms. So he no longer dances the separate parts of Chaos and Order, he doesn't act and live through the usual patterns and alternations of Nature.

The Dragon is not forced by any law to reenter the world. And yet, the Gate is open—there's no door—so nothing prevents him from Returning to dualistic phenomena as a *continuation* of his Return to the Source.

He unceasingly makes this return flight, but for no *reason* other than to enjoy truly natural and complete respiration, a "full stretch" and "free breathing." The Dragon's "breathing" doesn't have any inherent restriction or *necessity* to "breathe in" after "breathing out," etc. His Yang expansions needn't be followed by Yin contractions (or vice versa).

So, the Dragon has none of the limits we normally consider fundamental or 'natural.' But his luxurious stretching and wriggling gesture doesn't represent a transcendence of our existence at all, only its essential character, fully exposed.

189

TWELVE

SECTION II: THE DRAGON'S GESTURE AS YOGA

Yogic traditions direct us toward realizing union with our original nature and our origin. In Taoist yoga, this union is central, but its expression or celebration is also important—our origin is thoroughly *alive* ('immortal'). TWELVE's immortal Dragon shows the most quintessential character of this yogic affirmation of life, even though yoga as *technique* has been outgrown.

From SEVEN onward, we relax into the yogic momentum in the human relationship to Nature. ELEVEN both fully realizes and resolves that momentum toward Union (in demonstrations such as the Body of Light). These demonstrations in turn serve as preliminary *examples* of the Dragon's on-going yogic gesture in TWELVE.

The one essential feature of this gesture is that the cultivator makes a complete Return, uniting with the Source and also—in our Dragon's freedom—'departing' again simultaneously. Thus, this ultimate gesture of refinement and distillation involves entering the Source to abide with It indissolubly. But the 'indissoluble' character of Returning to the Source is consistent with a return *to* the world. For instance, the Body of Light shows that *complete* Return to the Source means shedding and radiating *into* phenomena as a gesture *from the Source*— so we dissolve our nature in the Source and then "let it go" still further, in a sense, *back* to the 'world' (not necessarily just the human world).

The capability to do this at the end of ELEVEN essentially anticipates or requires the Dragon's power. The Body of Light and all Taoist yogic techniques thus illustrate the pervasive bi-directionality in our Return to the Source, and it is that dynamic tendency which is represented in the Dragon's flight at TWELVE.

This tendency might also be demonstrated at ELEVEN and TWELVE quite subtly, without any extraordinariness or drama. We needn't become preoccupied with *extraordinary* accomplishments like thwarting the process of physical decomposition at death. The important point is just to live and die in a way that contributes to a *complete* experience of Return.

It's very common for so-called 'meditative' practice to be somewhat incomplete or top-heavy, leaving the body out of what is mistakenly perceived as a primarily mental process. Such approaches are also rather transcendence-oriented. They're motivated by thinking that what is "of the world" is not important and can be 'dumped' on our way elsewhere. A better approach is to respectfully include such 'worldly' components in our cultivation and then properly shed or radiate them into one of the territories of our freedom. Taoist yogic practices exemplify that conception of cultivation.

We can metaphorically summarize the uncommonly concrete and *thorough* techniques of Taoism by saying that its yoga is about connecting to all that we are and then participating in the full cycle of Yin and Yang ... not to change or become special, but to become familiar with the real course and context of our existence. In the process, we further refine our sense of ourselves until we find a more direct movement—a yogic "dragon's path" which moves by itself—linking pure Yin and Yang nondualistically.

Traveling that central route or channel without any effort takes us through the Gate of Yin and Yang but also continues on, back to a center or Heart of phenomenal existence 'between' Yin and Yang. From there we radiate out into life, regulating, nurturing, supporting all functions. Eventually we die or enter the Dragon's action in other ways, returning our essence both to the living manifest universe and to its mysterious Source.

THE EYE OF THE DRAGON

The experience of being the Dragon, emerging from its egg, is connected to the rising prominence of another keen eye on the our situation, the Fifth Eye. Like the other 'eyes' we've discussed, the Fifth Eye really begins to open several Stages before it becomes stable and continuously operative. So its initial activation is generally simultaneous with that of the Fourth Eye in EIGHT.

Actually, the Third, Fourth, and Fifth Eyes are all fundamentally related. They're simply various, progressively more encompassing 'takes' on what we are—as we continue along the Way, there's just less and less 'blinking.'

The Fifth Eye finds the Source in its true relation to phenomena. It therefore puts a final, really mature perspective on the human relationship to Nature.

Monkey and Sage were both filled with self-importance until they reached a true assessment of themselves in SIX and were then dissolved in SEVEN. The Third Eye penetrated that illusion of importance, but also gives us a new quality of power deriving from openness. Consequently, people who stress the cultivation of the Third Eye may sometimes become stuck in it, unable to release their power. This subtle trap is avoided when a more complete picture of the Way's Stages is available.

We should let this concentrated personal power go, opening to the larger perspective and context of the luminous environment of the Fourth Eye. This Eye, in turn, may impart a majestic quality to our bearing and actions, making us seem like 'cosmic' rulers, commanding other beings and possessing vast knowledge of various realms. But with the full view of the Stages, this 'specialness' also fades and the utterly hidden or discrete quality of the Heavenly Hsien's *truly* universal action emerges.

The Fifth Eye then just closes the circle. It brings us back to the real import of humanness, and so makes us almost invisible, nothing special at all. With the union of this Eye and the energetic, physical, and other experiential facets of the Dragon's nature (which have always been inseparable aspects of our existence), we act *from the center*. We then really don't need to know or do anything specific in order to act on everything ... our existence "in the center" calls all peripheral supportive and implementing forces into play without our even noticing or intending it.

All command in the sense of regulating our relationship with other beings and with Nature is accomplished just by our ordinary presence. The pressure or burden of being extraordinary or intelligent is gone ... we completely trust the human relationship to Nature to take care of things.

The Fifth Eye is the fierce eye of the Dragon, who brooks no limitations or interference from anything. But it's also the ordinary eye of human beings. Together with the other facets of our living nature, it overpowers anything that obscures or diminishes the basic human relationship to Nature, as it is.

TWELVE

SECTION III: FINAL REFLECTIONS ON CULTIVATING THE WAY

The division of the Way into twelve portions, and our references to those portions as 'stages,' should not be taken to mean that the Way essentially depends on efforts, achievements, or real improvement over time. This point is made best by the Dragon at TWELVE.

The Dragon is not an ultimate attainment, but rather the Being quality of the Way and all of the 'stages.' TWELVE is not an end at all. It's the fullness of the other Stages in their real context—the Tao. TWELVE is thus the ground as well as the pinnacle of the Way, and the Dragon's movement shows that the Tao is not something apart from ordinary existence. It's not a heavenly or transcendent place, nor an overwhelming openness (as preliminary experience of SEVEN might suggest).

The issue has been to find what our existence encompasses, and all that that really requires is our creation … the rest unfolds naturally. The Stages we've identified are not arbitrary conventions—the Way truly does involve these twelve aspects. And it's the Way of Nature for these Stages to breathe into and through one another. It would only be presumptuous for us to think that we can achieve Return to the Source by some effort on our part, over and above what is already running in all directions through the fabric of existence.

The Tao simply creates the possibility of "coming to meet itself," of demonstrating all of its facets, through ordinary time, in which the integral character of our natures is itemized in a piecemeal fashion. 'Forging' the pieces then becomes the agenda, but only in a playful, appreciative way, without pretense or aggression ... we know from the start that nothing is really broken or needs improvement.

We do need to include everything, to participate and trust in our nature and in Nature. We may also feel the need to relax apparent divisions between ourselves and Nature. But even the motivation for these 'needs' is actually the Dragon character of each of us. The Dragon's flights through the Gate are perpetual movements that constitute the force of the entire Way.

What makes Monkey nervous in ONE is simply a rather compressed view of what the Dragon is (a view naturally permitted by the freedom inherent in our Being). TWELVE saturates Monkey and makes him frantic, pushing him back and forth across the branches, because his appreciation of that energy is incomplete and so he's uncomfortable.

In fact, Monkey's clinging to this discomfort and 'incompleteness' rather than staying within comfort, is itself really just another, radical way of demonstrating a nondual view! A similar point can be made for the other characters and Stages.

We cannot take the Dragon to be a supreme accomplishment because all the eleven Stages on 'our' side of the Gate of Duality *are* the Dragon. We are the Dragon moving toward the Gate without effort and we are also the Dragon returning through the Gate.

More generally, the apparent ordering of the Stages from ONE to TWELVE is only that—an appearance, a way of looking that corresponds to our initial approach. TWELVE shows that the Stages are all directly interconnected, without really being ordered as 'low' vs 'high,' 'early' vs 'late,' etc. Like Chaos, Nature is too open-ended to harbor preferences for one Stage over another.

TWELVE and its Image are ultimate only in being the best *summary* of the complete Way. They remind us that the other Stages too are a delightful Dragon's Play.

THOSE WHO ATTAIN

It's not essential to 'attain' one of the later stages. But it *is* important that we *are* on the Way, participating and circulating. Experiencing being at a particular Stage does not *rank* you, but places you in the context of the Way and Its movements, which is all these Stages.

If you see clearly that you're at TWO, and you understand that TWO is part of this whole picture (ONE through TWELVE), then you really appreciate where your life is happening, what it's connected to, what breathes through it. That's enough, because it puts your life in its real context.

So, if you find yourself anywhere within this view, then you experience your participation in the Way. The rest is a matter of personal affinities in the huge sweep of Nature, and there are no winners or losers in that relationship, just people demonstrating different parts of it. The Way is not a "means to an end" of any sort. You may realize your position and not care about striving to examine the other Stages ... that's fine, even appropriate, perhaps.

Be in your life, appreciate the part *you're* playing. Remember that, above all else, you're already a Dragon.

About the Authors

Charles E. Belyea has studied traditional Chinese medicine for over twenty years, and serves as a health consultant in dietetics as well as a lecturer in Chinese History and Philosophy. He holds a degree in Asian Aesthetics from Antioch College, with a concentration on the role of ceramics in the traditional Tea Ceremony of China and Japan. He has also explored the application of Asian architectural principles (geomancy/feng shui) to enhance the experience of modern life, with special emphasis on the creation of harmonious contemplative communities.

His study of meditation began in 1966, and included work with Chinese, Tibetan, and Japanese teachers. While training in Taiwan, he was ordained as a Buddhist monk, and taken by his patron to visit many of the island's retreat hermitages. This led to his meeting and apprenticing with several Taoist masters, including the patriarch of an ancient family lineage of Yogic Taoism. Upon receiving the qualifications to teach this tradition, he returned to the United States and undertook a long solitary retreat. He then initiated his collaboration on instructional books with Mr. Tainer, and founded the Da Yuen Circle of Yogic Taoism in the United States. He also acted as the Founding Director of the Five Branches Institute in Santa Cruz. He has since spent several years on sabbatical in Indonesia and Malaysia, frequently returning to Mainland China and Taiwan. He now divides his time between Asia and California.

Steven A. Tainer is a professional writer and teacher, now concentrating on the direct experience and expression of key insights offered by Taoism and Buddhism. After completing his academic training in the Philosophy of Science in 1970, he embarked on a more experiential exploration, involving full-time study of Buddhist Epistemology and Logic with Tibetan lamas. He taught a variety of courses in this area, while writing many related books and articles. In 1981 he met Mr. Belyea and began an eleven-year process of retraining to digest the Taoist View of life and integrate it into ordinary circumstances. Throughout much of the 1980's, he also managed departments in several areas of the computer graphics industry. In 1989–90 he took a writer's sabbatical and meditation retreat, working with Mr. Belyea to produce both *Dragon's Play* and other manuscripts on Taoism. He is also investigating new approaches to mathematics education (1992–93 publications). His hobbies are walking, juggling, eating with friends in restaurants, and enjoying life's paradoxes.

Messrs Belyea and Tainer now offer a range of Da Yuen Circle programs, emphasizing basic, practical spirituality for contemporary life. Please write to the publisher, Great Circle Lifeworks, if you wish information concerning these courses or other related books or tapes by the authors.

Xiao-Lun Lin is a classically-trained artist from Guangzhou province in Mainland China. He specializes in ink brush paintings of birds and flowers, as well as in calligraphy. He has held several exhibitions in San Francisco and the Sunnyvale area. A graduate of San Jose State University, he currently teaches painting at the Japanese Culture Center, Foothill College.